Blur

Editor: **Mike Evans**
Assistant Editor: **Michelle Pickering**
Production Controller: **Michelle Thomas**
Picture Research: **Emily Hedges**
Art Editor: **Ashley Western**
Design: **Design Revolution**

First published in 1995 by
Hamlyn, an imprint of
Reed Consumer Books Limited,
Michelin House, 81 Fulham Road,
London SW3 6RB
and Auckland, Melbourne, Singapore and Toronto

Blur

PAUL LESTER

HAMLYN

CONTENTS

Early Life   5

Single Life   15

Leisure Life   29

Dark Life   43

Mod Life   57

Park Life   71

★★★★★☆★☆★★★★★★★

Early Life

COME TOGETHER

BLUR weren't always Blur. It's hard to imagine now, so central a part do they play in our pop lives, but once upon a time, way back in some long-forgotten pre-modern age – 1989, to be precise – when bands with odd names like The Stone Roses and Happy Mondays ruled the earth (or, at least, Britain)

Damon Albarn's bohemian childhood in suburban Essex and his father's psychedelic history ... he discovers Two Tone and early Eighties pop ... Damon meets Graham Coxon in school ... heads for London ... joins theatre school, forms synth-duo and enters University ... meets Alex James and Dave Rowntree, forms Seymour, who soon become Blur...

and a strange northern town called Manchester was considered to be the centre of the universe, Blur were not the group we know and love today. They were, in fact, called Seymour.

It was an inauspicious name for an inauspicious start to a highly auspicious career. Seymour were Blur in all but name

and musical style. Different approach, same members. And who were the guilty men? Stand up Damon Albarn, Graham Coxon, Alex James and Dave Rowntree.

Seymour's mainman Damon Albarn had an interesting family history. His father, Keith, put on Yoko Ono's first art exhibition and was involved with late Sixties, psychedelic-era, jazz-rock experimentalists Soft Machine, who featured the unique vocals of drummer Robert Wyatt before the literally crippling accident which left him wheelchair-bound (Wyatt, not Damon's old man). Albarn senior was trained as an artist and was Soft Machine's resident conceptual stage designer – he created then built an early prototype of interactivity, the indoor 'happening centre' known as the 'Discotheque Interplay', on the beach at Saint-Aygulf, southern France, in 1967's Summer of Love.

Clearly, Keith Albarn's wayward artistic genes were passed on to his son. In the year before Damon's birth (on March 23rd, 1968), as *Record Collector* explained in their July 1994 issue, Soft Machine played a five-day beer festival which was eventually shut down by the Mayor of St Tropez because, as said public servant apparently exclaimed, 'I don't want that pig-sty in my house!' The 'Discotheque Interplay' was closed down for spurious reasons of safety.

Until he was 10, Damon lived in the less than salubrious Leytonstone, on the

Blur's synthpop heroes, The Human League

outskirts of east London. Then, after a six-month period living in Turkey, the Albarns upped sticks to Colchester, Essex, where Keith landed a post running the local art school. Colchester was probably even less glamorous and exciting a location than Leytonstone. In fact, after Blur's initial rush of success in early 1991, several local papers ran furious cover stories based around Damon's less than favourable comments on his former hometown.

'Places like Colchester are stifling, and they celebrate the mediocre,' he told *Select* magazine in 1991. 'I don't really have any fond memories of the place at all.'

The response in Colchester was hardly cool, and the band were even wary about performing there one night for fear of retribution from angry, beered-up Essex lads and ladettes.

Notwithstanding the suburban normality of his surroundings, Damon's homelife was rarely ordinary. Damon – who was spied by *Vox* magazine casually smoking dope in front of his dad, backstage after a Blur gig – recalled his unconventional, 'bohemian' childhood with fondness in the now-defunct *Rage* magazine when he said: 'I was always mixing with interesting people who were prepared to talk to me. I was never treated as a child, I was always treated as a young adult. I think my earliest memory is living in our house near the forest and just sitting among the rhododendrons and walking through the trees. There was a monastery nearby with a silent sect of monks who I used to watch every morning.'

In 1979, the precocious Albarn first entered secondary school, Colchester's Stanway Comprehensive. Within a year, he had met future Seymour/Blur guitarist Graham Coxon, who was born in Germany on March 12th, 1969, and was therefore in the year below at school. It has to be said the pair's initial encounter wasn't quite as cataclysmic as it might have been.

'They're not proper brogues,' an obnoxious, 12-year-old Albarn said to a shy, retiring, 11-year-old Coxon, approaching him during a school trip and pointing at his footwear. And so there began a musical partnership that would one day take them, as The Beatles once put it, 'to the toppermost of the poppermost'.

Damon and Graham soon discovered they had many things in common, from the highbrow (playing instruments, watching Mike Leigh's *Meantime*) to the middlebow (listening to The Jam, early Eighties electro-pop outfits and 'Two Tone' bands such as Madness and The Specials) to the decidedly lowbrow (snogging girls). They were also both promising classical musicians who regularly had their compositions performed by the Essex Youth Orchestra. Graham taught himself to play both saxophone and guitar, while Damon was a budding pianist who even managed to write a score that won one of the regional heats of 'Young Composer Of The Year'.

By the mid-Eighties, the duo, now in their mid-teens, had left school (it was apparently later burned down – by a teacher who was angered to the point of arson because he was overlooked for the deputy headship!). Coxon had gone off to Colchester Art College while Albarn opted for a drama school called East 15 with a penchant for method acting. Pretty soon, Albarn was being asked by his lecturers to live rough, or to spend long periods pretending to be notorious Middle-Eastern totalitarian dictators.

'Yeah, I was given assignments like becoming a tramp for two months and being the Ayatollah . . . and having to steep myself in those worlds,' he remembers with very little affection.

After his brief flirtation with acting, the singer took his entire life savings (the princely sum of £2,000) and moved to London where he hung out at art exhibitions and formed a synth duo called Two's A Crowd with an accomplice known only as Sam. Little is known about this particular musical venture, and evidently Damon has tried to disown it, which is why, unfortunately, the rumour about Damon performing mime artist routines onstage with Two's A Crowd must remain – perhaps forever – unconfirmed.

However, in May 1991 *Smash Hits* did manage to dig out an old photo of Two's A Crowd for a mini-feature cruelly entitled: 'Tee-Hee! It's Damon From Blur In A Previous Pop Life!' The piece describes the duo as 'techno', while the carefully posed picture of Damon (standing next to 'Sam'), all baggy jeans and spiky hair, one arm raised triumphantly in the air, the other seemingly twiddling away on a keyboard, suggests Two's A Crowd were descendants of that proud lineage of photogenic, stylised electro-twosomes such as Blancmange, Erasure, Tears For Fears and Soft Cell.

'Good lord!' cried *Smash Hits* at the end of the article.

Good lord indeed.

LESS IS SEYMOUR

WHILE Damon was with Two's A Crowd, he secured a part-time job in a recording studio called the Beat Factory. By day, he worked at

Psychedelic voyagers Pink Floyd with Sultan of Strange Syd Barrett *(far right)*

Damon Albarn at his most blissed out and baggy

Le Croissant in Euston Station, while by night he was tea boy-cum-developing artist at the Beat. Pretty soon, Albarn started work on his own material, including future Blur tracks such as 'Birthday' (later to appear on Blur's debut album, 'Leisure'). He also found time to take a course at Goldsmith's College in New Cross, part of the University of London in the south-east of the city.

It was at Goldsmith's that Damon hooked up with Graham Coxon once again and Seymour/Blur began to take shape. Graham had embarked on a Fine Art degree, and before long he met student of French and future Blur bassist Alex James (born in Bournemouth, November 21st, 1968), soon to be described by *Sky* magazine as 'the most beautiful man in pop'. By 1988, Graham had introduced Damon to Alex, and together with 'Uncle' Dave Rowntree – a computer engineer, a part-time (in his words) 'agit-prop-Marxist-red flag-squat-

punk with a blond mohican' and occasional drummer who was born in Colchester on April 8th, 1963, and who Graham had previously been in bands with back home – the four started rehearsing.

(If Blur's August 1991 interview with *Melody Maker*'s Everett True is to be believed, there was an interim period between leaving college and forming the band for the four young lads. Apparently, Alex James spent the time 'helping to rebuild a nuclear power station', Dave had various 'executive, sitting-behind-desks, high-powered jobs', Graham 'worked in Sainsbury's for a couple of months' then 'worked in a pea-picking plant as a human combine harvester' while Damon 'worked on a fruit farm where he got to drive the tractor one day, decided to do a wheelie and got the sack'. Strange boys.)

By summer 1989, the group had a name – Seymour, a fictional creation of Damon's

warped imagination – a four-dimensional presence – Damon the cocky frontman, Graham his wasted sidekick, Alex the louche lothario and Dave the diamond geezer – and had already played several gigs around the capital. They were yet to have a record deal or receive any reviews from the music papers, although later articles did give some idea of what Seymour were actually like at this time.

'Damon was hunched over a mini-keyboard, plinking out an insane piece of [Erik] Satie-esque doggerel, while the others built and demolished a wall of noise that caught the ear,' reminisced the *Sounds* journalist Leo Finlay a year after Seymour's first show. 'Their set was astonishingly tight and imaginitive for a debut gig,' Finlay went on, 'and even the headline act the New Fast Automatic Daffodils – probably the only British act who can touch them live – found it hard to follow.'

Graham Coxon gives it some mad axe mania

One early review described Seymour as 'wacky', comparing them to Irish japesters Five Go Down To The Sea. In November 1990, Damon told *Sounds*, 'We were a manic, completely unfocused version of what we are now.' In the same interview, Alex James said, 'We were the maggot that turned into a butterfly!' and remembered Seymour as 'just this big esoteric thing,' a point borne out by the three bonus tracks

that appeared alongside Blur's 'Sunday Sunday' single of 1993.

'Dizzy', 'Fried' and 'Shimmer' all date back to 1989 and offer a rare glimpse of Seymour's eclectic, not to mention chaotic, musical approach. 'Dizzy' has echoes of late Sixties psychedelia as well as of post-punk innovators such as XTC and Gang Of Four. 'Fried' is a frantic burst of New Wave noise, while 'Shimmer' is a feedback-drenched riff

without a tune over which Damon's electronically treated, reverb-laden vocals mumble incomprehensibly.

The first track predates the sort of meandering curios to be found on the 'Leisure' album, the second predates the so-called New Wave Of New Wave scene of 1994 while the third predates Blur's later predilection for Syd Barrett-era Pink Floyd whimsy. Some of this stuff was pretty heavy.

It's no surprise, then, that, for one gig, Seymour supported apocalyptic, sampladelic metal-bashers, Switzerland's Young Gods.

Fate intervened in November 1989 when, just before a Seymour gig at London's Dingwalls, Food Records supremo Andy Ross, who had heard the band were a dynamic live proposition and wanted to see for himself, was prevented from entering the venue. 'The bouncer wouldn't let me in,' he recalls. Ross was even more determined to see the band several weeks later at Islington's Powerhaus. He was fairly impressed – 'They were crap, but entertaining,' he told *Vox* – although this wasn't his first experience of Seymour.

'They had already sent me a demo tape of four songs,' Ross told *Record Collector*. 'One of them was "She's So High" [Blur's debut single], another one was "Fool" [a track from "Leisure"], and there were two other tracks that were arty and shambolic and not particularly inspiring at all. But the two better tracks showed they had a clear grasp of the facets of simple songwriting. Everything was in its right place and in the right proportion.'

THERE'S NO OTHER NAME

WELL, almost everything. Food bosses Ross and Dave Balfe (formerly of early Eighties Liverpudlian avant-popsters, Teardrop Explodes) agreed to sign the band, who scribbled on the dotted line in March 1990, just as Graham and Alex's finals were approaching (the delinquent rockers bunked off their exams and failed to finish their degrees, the naughty pair claiming their college peers were either 'cunts or posers'). There was one essential condition before Food opened their coffers, however: the name Seymour had to go.

'We just weren't interested in signing a band called Seymour,' Ross explains. 'It was a crap name – too airy-fairy.'

So Ross and the band came up with Blur, in hindsight a far better name than Seymour, which Damon once claimed was generously bequeathed to them by 'someone in an anorak'. In their first ever cover story in the April 6th, 1991, issue of *Melody Maker*, Steve Sutherland extolled the virtues of Blur's exceedingly appropriate name, asking: 'Was there ever a band more aptly named? Blur. It's perfect. Blur are all over the place, a blast, a brilliant shambles.' 'I don't think our name sounds like some-one being sick. It

My Bloody Valentine – doyens of experimental noisepop

sounds more like someone burping,' joked Damon in *Smash Hits*. He was more serious in the 'inkies': 'Blur is just a good name, and you need that for getting into the press,' he told *Sounds* in July 1990, and he was right – within five months of signing to Food, Blur were already receiving lots of music press attention, most of it a taste of the hyperbolic purple prose to come.

'Blur are London's latest and most precociously vibrant live affront,'gushed one journalist at the time. 'Breathtaking,' sighed another, going on to assert that comparisons between Blur and The Stone Roses and My Bloody Valentine were fair in that all three bands were capable of 'writing classic pop tunes and turning them into dynamite live'.

But it wasn't just the hacks who were singing Blur's praises – the band were more than capable of issuing outrageous proclamations on their own. It wasn't long before the world became aware of Blur's, and in particular Damon's, tendency to utter statements and make claims that teetered on that narrow line between the confident and the downright arrogant.

Not only did Albarn invoke the spirit of the Theatre Of Cruelty of the 1930s ('I like things to repulse people, to upset and move them,' he told *What's On* magazine. 'I don't want to give people an identity, I want to give them a crisis'), he also stressed Blur's fearsome live demeanour, implying their onstage antics were far more threatening and dangerous than their 'baggy' peers such as The Soup Dragons and The Mock Turtles, bands that seemed content to look half-asleep during gigs, all floppy fringes and comatose presence.

In *Select*, Damon, without the slightest hint of self-consciousness, stated: 'I've always known I'm incredibly special.' Then, in an exchange with George Berger of *Sounds*, the singer, flushed with bravado, exclaimed: 'I wouldn't bother if I didn't think we were the best band in the universe.'

'Better than the Sex Pistols, the Rolling Stones and The Beatles?' asked the gobsmacked journalist.

'I think over a 10-year period we will be, yeah,' was Albarn's considered, and immodest, reply.

Blur's supernatural belief in their own abilities extended to their musical and compositional skills as well as to their commercial viability.

'The difference between Seymour and Blur,' Damon once said, 'is that Blur are going to be hugely successful. It's inevitable that we're going to sell loads of records.' Of their contemporaries, he added: 'There's no interest in the current music scene for us. I don't have any records and I'm not interested in any other bands.'

Notwithstanding Albarn's claims for his band's musical originality and assertions of independence from the past/his peers, many were quick to draw parallels between Blur's sound and that of others.

'If The Stone Roses are The Beatles and Happy Mondays are the Stones, then Blur are The Who,' decided one writer, acknowledging Blur's raw power and high energy as well as Damon's manic presence. Meanwhile, the wall-of-guitars of Echo & The Bunnymen, the melodies of The Beatles, the indie-dance grooves of The Stone Roses, the quintessential Englishness of The Kinks, the psychedelic experiments of Pink Floyd and the noise innovations of My Bloody Valentine were offered by desperate hacks as explanations for How Blur Got Their Sound.

Live, Blur were, by all accounts, fast, furious, ferocious, crazed, demonic, charged, cathartic, explosive, rabid, rough, raw. In fact, several promoters were said to be getting a bit nervous whenever Albarn's Army turned up to chuck themselves around their venues.

As Albarn admitted to *Sky* magazine: 'I like injuries.'

Indeed, the following April, Blur were banned from performing at the Woughton Centre in Milton Keynes after a schoolboy in the audience suffered head injuries during their set – Alex James allegedly dived offstage into the crowd, still clutching his guitar, and collided with the fan, who later needed stitches to a head wound.

Damon Albarn told *NME*: 'We're not a mad, irresponsible band. Our gigs don't usually end up in a blood-bath.'

That said, according to the *NME*'s Simon Williams, promoters at London's Borderline, Powerhaus and Brixton's Academy were starting to visibly shudder at the mention of Blur's name.

Back in late '91, Damon told Williams: 'A lot of the venues have got really pissed off with us, like really emotional about it all, saying, "We have much bigger bands than you playing here all the time and none of them behave like you!" That just shows how staid it all is if it's such a shock to see someone doing things like that.'

Things like what? According to *Melody Maker*'s Push, Damon was busy doing daft and dangerous stuff along the lines of: 'hurling himself around the stage, tumbling into the audience, scrambling onto the bassist's shoulders, swinging from the rafters like a drunken chimp and leaping into the air time and time again, more often than not landing flat on his backside. These antics have to be seen to be believed. At one point, he accidentally rips open his hand and smears the blood all over his face.'

Iggy who?

Blur (1991) demonstrating high-rise cred

Single Life

'HIGH' ANXIETY

SO Blur had proved themselves as a vital, volatile live act. But the question was, could they cut it on record?

In October 1990, we found out. The band's debut single, 'She's So High', was released in the second week of that month to reasonable public interest – it peaked at Number 48 in the charts – and to much critical acclaim. *NME* and *Sounds* both made gave it the highly-coveted Single Of The Week award, the former, in typically confused and confusing (for the *NME*, anyway) rock journalese, praising its 'instant sugar-hit swirly riff, daydreamer vocals and incense wafts of backwardly winding effects', the latter going so far as to claim 'it stands comparison with anything made in the last five years', describing Blur as 'the first great band of the Nineties'.

The *Sounds* man may have been right in his second pronouncement, but his first was arguable, to say the least. As debut singles go, 'She's So High', according to Damon a 'wanting-sex-song' ('She's so high/I want to crawl all over her,' went the chorus) about an unattainable female goddess figure, was pretty good, although hardly worthy of inclusion in the hallowed pantheon of Explosive Opening Salvos that includes The Sex Pistols' 'Anarchy In The UK', The Smiths' 'Hand In Glove', Frankie Goes To Hollywood's 'Relax', New Order's 'Ceremony', ABC's 'Tears Are Not Enough', or even, gallingly enough as far as Damon is concerned, Suede's 'The Drowners' (about which, more later – see chapter four).

No, 'She's So High' was just OK. The best record of the last five years, though? Be serious. It's in the Top 500 – maybe. Far less fast and furious than Blur live, it remains a record of its time, a half-assed attempt at creating a lazy, languid, libidinous dance sound, Damon's dazed'n'confused vocals, Graham's fazed guitar effects and honeyed harmonies as well as the stoned, loping beat all sounding very 1990.

'I Know', one of the other tracks (Blur have always been generous with B-sides and additional songs on singles – at last count, there have been 47 extra tracks on the various formats of Blur's 12 single releases), is Blur's very own contribution to the indie-dance oeuvre (see also: The Stone Roses' 'Fools Gold', Happy Mondays' 'Wrote For Luck' and The Charlatans' 'The Only One I Know'), while 'Down' features the vaguest of vague melodies rambling nowhere very slowly and offers an early example of Graham Coxon's soon-to-be-celebrated guitar hero pyrotechnics.

The last few months of 1990 saw Blur consolidating their live reputation, heading out on a 21-date tour of average-size venues and the usual Polytechnics/Universities; receiving bigger and bigger music press features, full of yet more outrageous claims by journalists and outlandish self-aggrandisement on the part of the band; crossing that treacherous 'serious muso'/teen fan divide with their first ever pubescent mag articles ('Blur are shaggable! No question about it!' foamed *Rage* magazine in November of that year); and whipping up considerable controversy with the sleeve of 'She's So High'.

HIPPO CRITS

WHATEVER you think of Blur's music, there is little denying their records have great sleeves. The front cover of 'She's So High' featured a tiny image multiplied 12 times, taken from a well known Sixties painting by Mel Ramoff. It was also used by the band for T-shirts and a concurrent promotional poster campaign. Very colourful, very kitsch, very Pop Art.

And very sexist. Apparently. Many reckoned the picture of a naked woman,

D ebut single 'She's So High' reaches Number 48 in the charts ... their second single 'There's No Other Way' gets to Number Eight – 'Top Of The Pops' at last! ... first band front cover – Melody Maker ... Graham reveals himself something of a raving monster loony ...

Damon gives the author a lesson in French kissing

leaning forward provocatively, legs akimbo, on top of a yawning hippopotamus, was appallingly un-PC and responded accordingly. In November 1990, all three music weeklies contained news stories about the band's run-in with protesters at various British halls of learning.

According to *Sounds*, Blur got into pretty hot bother in Coventry Polytechnic's Steve Biko Bar, where they soon discovered that the Student Union had banned their new T-shirt on the grounds that it was offensive to women. Anyone wearing the sensibility-abusing garment, announced a missive from on high, would immediately be ejected from the Poly gig. In addition, the band were not allowed to sell their posters on the premises.

That same week, up at Warwick University, angry feminists attacked the merchandise stand at a Blur gig, charging the stall and ripping down posters. Meanwhile, the band's management started

receiving letters of complaint from Hackney Council in London about the sexist nature of the art work, while several posters in Brixton were defaced by feminist activists.

Not every female on the planet was incensed by the sleeve, however. Typical was one sarcastic correspondent to *Melody Maker*'s letters page who wrote: 'Grow up, you stupid little feminists! Everyone knows that girls have tits, so one little drawing won't make any difference.'

In defence, Damon Albarn said at the time: 'We're not sexist. I can't understand why there's all this fuss. It's a joke - surely that's obvious from the fact that it's got a hippopotamus on it.'

Sexist or not, the Hippo Affair – as it would never actually be called – pointed towards one inescapable conclusion: this band were rock-literate and playful, able to toy with the form – pop music – at their whim and disposal.

Clearly, they were also miles removed from the thuggish laddishness of many of their peers. From the start, it was obvious that Blur were erudite and articulate in a medium normally renowned for its

Erudite, articulate and charming

Jacuzzi does it !

monosyllabic moronicism. In their first major interview, in the November 10th issue of *Melody Maker*, The Stud Brothers celebrated Damon's familiarity with the works of Herman Hesse, Lobsang Rampa

Michael Caine, dead ringer for Damon?

and Albert Camus, going on to describe Albarn as 'intellectually arrogant'.

A later *Melody Maker* feature, written by the author of this book, tried to summarise the appeal of these highly qualified, charming middle-class men who seemed to have an acute understanding of working-class culture.

'Blur are not lads,' said this writer (echoing Damon's own statement weeks earlier to *Sky* magazine: 'I hate machismo, it's preposterous'). 'Apart from Dave, who fits most neatly into the regular geezer category, arch-epicurean Alex is like a character from *Brideshead Revisited*, Graham is a hedonistic, self-destructive pretty boy while Damon reminds me of Hywel Bennett in some Technicolor mid-Sixties film, or Michael Caine in *Alfie*, half middle-class theatrical who's about to go "Daaahling!" at any moment, and half Cockney wideboy heartbreaker.'

From the beginning, Blur found they were able to straddle pop's numerous, and previously unnegotiable, divides: credible / shaggable, teen / twentysomething, kiddie mag / inkie, fun / serious, prole / student. They may well have known their French existentialists from their 'French Letters', but they also knew the classic pop trick of how to contrive a radio-friendly tune whose chorus could worm its way into the consciousness of the general public.

It was this multifaceted crossover potential that would, within a short three years, take Blur to the pole position as one of the most successful – both critically and commercially – bands in Britain.

'WAY' TO GO
But there was one tiny problem: after almost two years into their (eventually success) story, Blur had yet to make a more than merely decent record.

Following a Christmas '90 appearance at Brixton Academy supporting baggy chancers The Soup Dragons, and mid-way through another major British tour, Blur put out their second single. Released in April 1991 and backed up by a cheekily subversive, suburban 'Oxo' family pisstake video featuring a giant trifle and filmed in a 500-grand Georgian house, 'There's No Other Way' hardly scaled Elysian Peaks, and it still failed to convey the sheer kinetic excitement of the in-concert Blur. (Damon himself later described the single as 'monumentally bland, an exercise, a scam'.) But it was a considerable improvement on their debut.

Supported by three extra tracks – 'Inertia', another hazy, lazy, psychedelic ramble, the early Bowie/mod-ish 'Mr Briggs', and the rocky 'I'm All Over' – 'There's No Other Way' boasted an infectious melody, insidious groove and irresistible chorus.

Blur's second single not only received the now-to-be-expected critical garlands – 'A corking single which had every manjack of us grooving within seconds' (*NME*); 'An organ-bleeding, guitar-powered, post-psychedelic dancefloor and radio-friendly monster' (*Music Week*); 'Fab!' (*Smash Hits*) – it also succeeded in doing very well in the pop charts.

And it didn't just make it into the indie charts, either – although Blur are on Food, an offshoot of major label Parlophone, they have always been perceived as Definitively Indie. (Indeed, it was probably around Blur that 'indie' as we know and feel ambivalent about it today finally crystallised as a concept.) No, 'There's No Other Way' actually reached a high position in the proper, grown-up, big boys' charts, climaxing its progress at a very creditable Number 8 in May 1991.

Number 8 meant success at last for Blur, a band who have always been aware of the true implications of the verb 'to succeed' – *Top Of The Pops*.

Even when he was just a skinny, facetious runt at school ('I was exceptionally

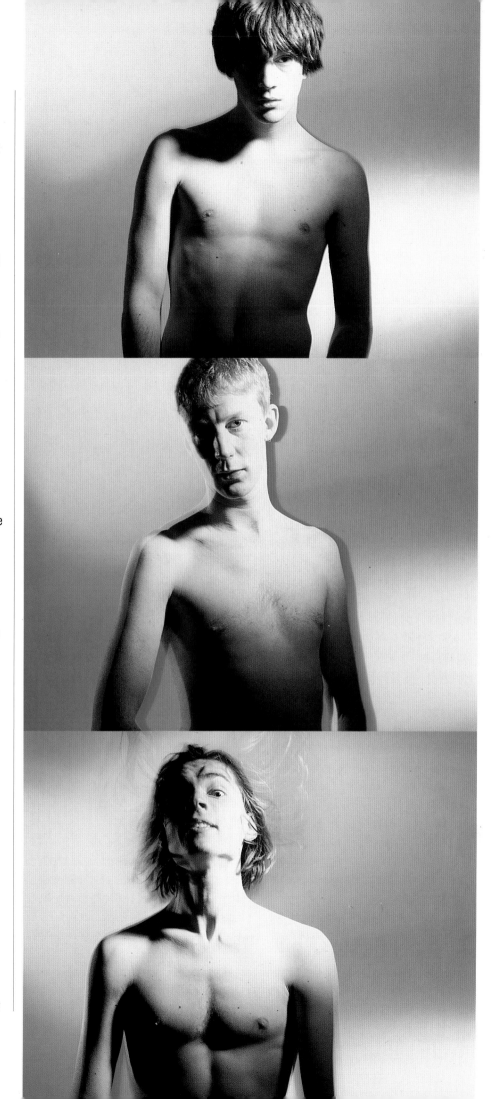

Blur: boys 'n' the hood

unpopular at school,' he once said. 'People thought I was a complete, big-headed, arrogant twat.'), Damon Albarn always suspected that, one day, he would make it on to *Top Of The Pops*.

'I've been preparing for this moment for years,' he told *Sky* magazine.

Steve Sutherland expanded on Albarn's adolescent megalomaniac tendencies in the band's first ever cover story, the issue of *Melody Maker* dated April 6th, 1991: 'Damon Albarn doesn't just think he will appear on *Top Of The Pops*. He doesn't just hope this will come to pass. He knows it. He believes it. Ever since he was 11, he's been sure that this is his destiny.'

Not that Damon himself approached the idea of appearing on the nation's premier frothy-pop show with anything less than utter gravity, as he explained to the *'Maker* in the above cover story. 'Being on *Top Of The Pops* for the first time is a massive

responsibility,' he said. 'It's a real honour. I mean, you're representing youth in front of this incredible audience of 10 million people and it's your duty to . . . put the knife in. That's the point when you should really start to become incredibly great. There can be no modesty. I don't believe in modesty when you're playing in front of 10 million people. I believe in just blossoming into something great, something . . .legendary.'

TEEN MACHINE

IN the wake of the chart success of 'There's No Other Way', Blur stopped being merely the cult darlings of the British music press and started becoming public property - bona fide kitten hunks to stir the fan-fixated imaginations / genitals of yer Sharons and Tracys in teen punterland.

Cue feverish interest from the weekly and monthly jailbait mags, as well as the Daily Sleazes of this world.

Now, Blur had already been called 'shaggable' by *Rage* magazine, but that was nothing compared to the torrent of sex-obsessed copy they generated after their first hit single.

'Busty girls and long-legged lovelies go wild for boozy band!' screamed the headline in the April 29th edition of the sensational, soaraway *Daily Star*, above a spurious, curious article which exposed to the nation precisely What Life Is Like In Blur.

'Life is one long round of birds and booze for the lads in Britain's number one groupie band – and they love it,' oozed the *Star*'s Linda Duff, her tongue apparently some considerable distance from her cheek as she revealed Blur's brand spanking new nicknames – 'Babe' (Damon), 'Cheesey' (Alex), 'The Quiet One' (Graham) and 'The Dark Destroyer' (Dave).

'The lads boast of boozing until they fall over, and regularly stage macho drinking contests,' the divine Ms Duff carried on, regardless. 'They even insist on travelling stark naked in the back of their tour van between gigs to prove they are all lads together. And their outrageous behaviour is earning them growing reputations as sex gods . . . Blur are young, sexy and wildly passionate about music and girls!'

Meanwhile, the pop mags were getting wildly passionate about Blur. *My Guy* hailed the arrival of Blur with this pithy piece of puerile prose: 'Meet Blur, four floppy-haired lads who just lurrrve snogging!' A few months later, they issued this startling revelation: 'Blur boy Damon Albarn wears the same pair of undies two days in a row.'

Gosh!

Next, in a series of daft articles before the magazine (surprisingly?) folded, *Number One* first re-christened our heroes 'Delectable Damon', 'Gorgeous Graham', 'Swoonsome Alex' and 'Desirable Dave'. Then they threw a slew of absurd questions at them: 'Do you know a good hang-over cure?'; 'Which side of the bed is best to sleep on?'; 'How do you make a good cup of tea?'. Finally, they detailed all manner of ridiculous paraphernalia such as: 'Alex is obsessed with whiffy French cheeses!'; 'Graham never brushes his hair'; Damon is a wild dancer and often hits himself on the head'; 'Alex has a scar on his right knee – he was bitten by a bulldog when he was in the cubs.'

Smash Hits were equally enthusiastic about the band they termed 'the new messiahs of anorak rock' (whatever that meant), compiling a lengthy fact-sheet entitled '40 Mind-Expanding Things You Never Knew About Blur' and including a dizzyingly compelling series of informative titbits such as: Blur love snogging! Damon's favourite word is 'wonderful'! Graham's favourite word is 'aardvark'! Dave's mum is a chiropodist! Graham's voice is all sort of creaky! Damon's eyebrows meet in the middle and he smiles like a wolf! Dave's got the longest blond eyelashes in the history of the planet!

And so forth.

FEATURE CREATURES

WHILE the tabloids and the teenies were gushing forth gobbledegook, Blur were becoming a ubiquitous presence in those good old music press stand-bys, the gossip columns. Hardly a week would go by during spring/ summer '91

without a reference to such-and-such a member of Blur propping up the bar at some lugubrious central London watering hole.

Pretty soon, Blur were as famous for their extra-curricular activities as they were for their records – remember that, thus far, they had produced a grand total of two singles. And so, week in, week out, we would be entertained with lurid tales of Blur's latest exploits down at the Town & Country Club or Oxford Street's Syndrome (the hip indie kid niterie of the early Nineties where punters could rub shoulders with music press cognoscenti and the indie brat pack) as they drank themselves into oblivion and mingled with such semi-celebrities and indie club mainstays as Lush, Moose, Slowdive, Ride, Chapterhouse, Swervedriver, Revolver and Silverfish. Before long, this coterie of boozing buddies had been bequeathed a name by *Melody Maker* – The Scene That Celebrates Itself.

One typical gossip column entry, in the August 3rd *NME*, went: 'You can always rely

extreme behaviour. And we're not just talking beer here. As Alex James told *Vox* magazine at the height of the umpteenth Ecstasy-fuelled Summer of Love: 'We are all white, middle-class and earning a living doing what we want to do . . . It's pathetic, really, all of us constantly shoving chemicals down our throats and saying how much we love each other.'

And when this writer went on the road with the band in June 1991, he was

delight as he emerged, bedraggled, from a gaggle of teenage girls; 'I like it when the girls go, "Fuck me, fuck me, fuck me!"' decided the so-laidback-he's-horizontal Alex James, who I described as 'like a trendy young professor with a penchant for port' - and the sort of spontanous inter-band punch-ups that teeter on that fine line between the fraternal scuffle and the fratricidal scrap'.

Then there was Damon's inability to keep

'Six quid to see Blur ? Bloody rip-off mate!'

Graham goes all surreal

on Blur to vomit half-masticated Big Macs and cheap drugs at the back of otherwise non-eventful gigs.'

At this point, Blur's taste for intoxicants was just amusing copy-fodder – it would be some months before their drinking became a serious issue. For now, their barfly impressions merely served to provide background colour for the numerous features that appeared after the success of 'There's No Other Way'. However, even this early on, Blur were showing signs of

surprised – make that 'startled' – by their bacchanalian, corybantic capacity for excess.

'We've got whisky, gin, vodka, brandy, Southern Comfort, light ale and lager,' the barman of a Bristol hotel offered one group member, probably Graham Coxon, as we relaxed in the lounge after a gig, only to be met with the response, uttered in complete seriousness, 'I'll have all of that.'

Elsewhere, your reporter noted scenes of wild abandon – 'I've just been snogged! I've just been snogged!' Graham squealed with

his opinionated comments and sardonic neo-Wildean witticisms below Very Loud on the decibel-o-meter, particularly whenever the band and I happened to find ourselves within earshot of hairy, Cro-Magnon types. This bizarre tendency was later sent up on a regular basis in *Melody Maker*'s satirical section, 'TTT', under the headline: 'Each Week, Damon From Blur Gets The Rest Of The Band Beaten Up'.

Most astonishing of all were Graham Coxon's no-holds-barred revelations to me on the band's tour bus on the journey between Bristol and Ipswich. I had already described Coxon as 'self-destructive'. Here, Blur's guitarist upped the ante with some serious psychotic reactions. It would seem worth repeating most of our conversation now, not least for the insight it offers into the mind of a member of one of the country's best-known bands, and a band often mistakenly perceived as vacuous, bumptious fun-merchants.

doesn't help cos you have to drink and smoke all the time.

'I was on a ferry with my old girlfriend around the same time,' he went on, 'and I'd bought these Gitanes, and they were killing me. And I dropped to the floor and started going a bit unconscious, and my girlfriend – who was bulimic, by the way – was just kicking me and going, "Get up, Graham! Stop showing me up!" And I was lying on the threshold of the toilet, and people were

and I sat against the wardrobe, and I just started bashing my head against it till I started getting fuzzy vision.

'Another time, we all went out and I got really drunk on champagne and Jim Beam and found myself walking in the middle of Notting Hill with no hope of getting home. And then I got run over. I don't know how the fucking hell it happened, really. I just ran into the road and got biffed up in the air by this car. It was really fucking hilarious. I was

Damon and Graham in phallic action

Damon giving it the Unplugged treatment

'I went to a mental hospital for two weeks once,' he started. 'But I wasn't mental, I was in the only normal ward in Colchester. There were all these old men wandering around with two miles of ash hanging off their fags – they were great, they'd go out and get me Superkings.

'I had anaemia, see. It was great. I had ulcers, too. I got them on the last tour with The Soup Dragons – I was clinging on to the seats, almost passing out with pain, and I was totally bleeding inside. Being in a band

just casually stepping over me.

'I'm attracted to trauma,' added Graham, as if he needed to. 'I like things like that. I'm a born martyr. Damon always says I'm like one of those old poets who carried handkerchiefs around with them and kept going into fits and saying, "Oooh, I'm feeling a bit giddy!"

'Do I scare people? Perhaps a bit. Alex does, too, although in a different way – he's just so laidback. I'm not. The other week, my current girlfriend was giving me a hard time,

brought to by this copper, and I just said, "Am I dead?"

'I had such an awesome time!' the guitarist continued, barely pausing for breath. 'I was living in these college halls, and when I went back there to see my girlfriend, Jane, I was concussed to fuck, I had blood on my face and I was limping and blabbering on about nothing. I had to be sedated. I was absolutely off my head. I started making sandwiches and cutting my fingers and there was blood everywhere.

Just amazing. . . sedation. . . wow.

'I've pretty much done everything I ever wanted to,' he decided, before offering this chilling conclusion to his rabid, livid stream-of-consciousness: 'I reckon I could die and I'd be happy. Yeah, I'd like to think I could commit suicide now . . .'

One can only wonder what *Smash Hits* would have made of that little lot.

LITTLE 'BANG' THEORY

IT was while watching the band at Bristol's Bierkeller, during the above on-the-road expedition, that I made the following observation about Blur.

Led Zeppelin – not as heavy as Blur. Allegedly.

'The band seem to thrive on a tension that at once pulls them close together and threatens to tear them apart. Blur are great, not in spite, but because of the chaos. Their music is crammed with metal guitar riffs worthy of Jimmy Page at his grungiest, maximum heaviosity Led Zep-ish drum breaks, Who-style chord detonations, dazed-and-confused Byrds-ian harmonies and ozone-hostile noise.

'"Birthday",' I gushed on (and on), 'is like Sonic Youth blazing a trail through The

Rolling Stones' "Fool To Cry", a gigantic rock ballad featuring huge piano fills . . . Blur's frictional meshing of black/white noise and colourful melodies is mirrored by the complex relationship between Damon's jolts of vitality, Alex's studied ennui (languor is his energy), Dave's steady rhythms and Graham's near-parody of shoegazing indie indifference.'

And yet, for all the fascinating facets of their live performances, Blur were still to deliver that all-important killer record. 'Bang', their third single, released in July 1991, was hardly What The World Was Waiting For. Faster than 'She's So High' and 'There's No Other Way', it still managed to sound lacklustre compared to the band's ferocious onstage attack. 'Bang' made it three lukewarm attempts in a row for Colchester's finest to contrive a mercilessly seductive dance groove. What a shame.

Meanwhile, the three additional tracks – 'Explain', featuring Damon's now patented cocky, faux-Cockney vocals; 'Luminous', a fairly tasty slice of cod-psychedelia, all breathy harmonies and shimmering Hammond sounds; and the 'Tomorrow

Blur get blurred

Never Knows'-era, Beatles-esque backwards effects of 'Beserk' – only just managed to alleviate one's sense of disappointment that Blur had yet to prove themselves as a formidable recording unit.

For all that, 'Bang' reached Number 24 in August, which meant a second *Top Of The Pops* appearance – this time, Damon did his best to confound and delight a nation's pop kids by camping it up with a plastic chicken in his hand. And the critics loved 'Bang'. *NME* made it Single Of The Week, praising its 'hearty noise, amazingly upfront vocals and student union singalong chorus'. *Melody Maker* was even more effusive: '"Bang" teeters between the brash ("I don't need anyone") and the coquettish ("But a little love could make things better"), and tops every dry, disaffected verse with a blindingly gorgeous chorus.'

Would Blur's debut album be their first great contribution to Nineties pop culture?

'Cor! Phwoarr!' etc

★★★★★☆★★★★★★★★★★☆

Leisure Life

Success Or Bust

Debut album released, enters charts at Number Seven ... their Reading Festival performance is savaged ... debut gig in New York, on the other hand, is rapturously received ... Food Christmas Party at Brixton Academy ...

ALBUM RAP

'LEISURE', Blur's debut album, finally came out after much anticipation in late August 1991. The sleeve, another Stylorouge production, was promising enough in a kitschily colourful way. After the hippo ('She's So High'), the baby ('There's No Other Way') and the cockerels ('Bang') came the Fifties bathing beauty in her flowery plastic swimming cap and heavy make-up.

Meanwhile, 'Leisure''s inner sleeve contained a whole long list of thank yous to various industry personnel and journalists who helped give the band a leg-up on their

way to pop's summit (no, really, I couldn't, you're too kind – oh, all right, then. Ta very much). It also featured Damon Albarn's lyrics, which – depending on which report you believed – were carefully constructed by the singer after prolonged bouts of navel-gazing or hastily cobbled together in the studio minutes before recording.

Yup, Albarn's words ran the gamut of lovelorn, angst-ridden, purple rock poetry from the sublime

Damon reinvents the meaning of flower power

to the deliberately gorblimey. Perfect examples of the latter abound on 'Leisure': 'All you have to do/Just you be you' ('Slow Down'); 'Inside my head/There's nothing left/It's all been taken out' ('Come Together'); 'It's my birthday/No one here day/Very strange day/I think of you day/Go outside day/Sit in park day' ('Birthday').

But there are moments of lucidity, moments when Albarn eschews mimsy poesy and strives towards a more straightforward, confessional style of songwriting, when he attempts to say

something unforgettable about relationships, life, love, whatever: 'All these things/That I told you/I didn't mean at all . . . I'd forget you' ('Slow Down'); 'Do you want anything you ever wanted? . . . Do you love anyone you ever loved?' ('Bad Day'); 'I know that you want me to leave/I'm amazed at how cold you can be' ('Fool').

Music-wise, 'Leisure' was over 50 minutes long – good value for money until you perused the back cover and realised all three singles were here, as well as a couple of ancient Seymour demos – 'Fool',

'Birthday' – and old live Blur favourites such as 'Repetition', all of which were fairly respectably tarted up by Morrissey's producer, Stephen Street.

As debut albums go, 'Leisure' wasn't bad. Unlike Primal Scream's 'Screamadelica', however, which was also released in late 1991 and was a double-album which offered a near-perfect confluence of rave and rock styles, Blur's guitar-dance efforts such as 'She's So High' and 'Come Together' demonstrated a rather less seamless alliance of two opposing cultures.

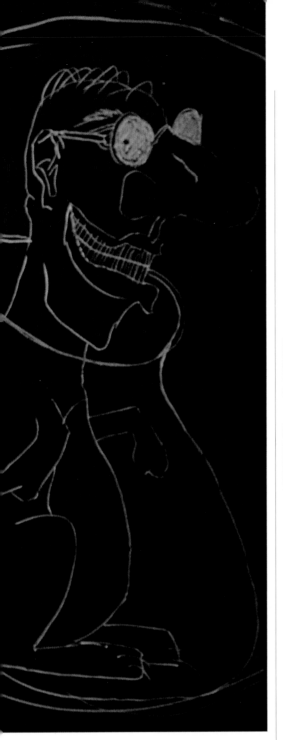

('Repetition') and mellifluous aural washes the likes of which proliferated on *NME*'s infamous monument to winsome jangles, the 'C86' cassette (see: 'Bad Day').

There were signs of interesting future developments, however. Closing track 'Wear Me Down' was formed around a fuzzy, grinding Hendrixy riff and plaintive chord sequence. 'Birthday' was an ultra-stoned, blissed-out delight that suggested Blur's chemical and/or pharmacological intake was increasing by the day. Best of all was the beautifully unnerving 'Sing', a six-minute mantra based around an unsettling series of spooky piano chords over which Damon intoned darkly about how there's no worth in anything 'if the child in your head is dead' – 'Sing' was proof positive, if it were needed, that Blur were already keen and ready to explore new musical terrains.

As David Cavanagh said in *Select*: 'Blur have declared their intention to get highly experimental and weird.' Without question, much of 'Leisure' made for pretty uneasy listening, and it would have come as no surprise to learn that punters allured by the

Graham, Damon, Dave and Alex, August 1991

Certainly, 'Leisure' was derivative. But then, so were later Blur LPs 'Modern Life Is Rubbish' and 'Parklife'. Unlike Blur's second and third albums, however, on 'Leisure' there was little evidence of the band doing interesting things with their influences.

Nowadays, Graham Coxon describes 'Leisure' as their 'indie detox album', on which they exorcised all their 'Dinosaur, Valentines and C86 bile', a reference to the LP's Dinosaur Jr-style grungy American guitar sounds ('Slow Down', say), spacey effects à la My Bloody Valentine

hummable groovability of 'She's So High' and 'There's No Other Way' were forced to stay away in their droves by some of 'Leisure''s more inaccessible moments.

What was surprising, therefore, was the fact that, in early September 1991, 'Leisure' entered the album charts at Number 7.

WHAT THE PAPERS SAID

SO the public liked it. But what did the critics think of 'Leisure'?

They loved it – most of them, anyway. In *Melody Maker*, Steve Sutherland described 'Leisure' as 'a promotional item par excellence, not so much an album as an advertisement for Blur. It pays heed to its time (the drums are often baggy, there's feedback and sustain) but, more importantly, it aspires to timelessness.' Concluded Sutherland: 'Blur will be the first of the new breed to be chauffeured around in day-glo Rolls Royces.' The monthlies were equally keen. In *Select*, long-term Blur supporter

David Cavanagh (who wrote the band's first ever page feature in April 1990, for the now sadly defunct *Sounds*) gave the album five-out-of-five squares, hailed the arrival of burgeoning guitar supremo Graham Coxon ('Come on, man, into the light, let the audience see you') and praised the bass-playing of Alex James who 'wrestles the sacred word "bassline" from the techno wilderness and reclaims it for the bass guitar – sheer bliss for the woofer contingent.' Cavanagh went on to celebrate the numerous gorgeous harmonies ('More "ooohs" and "aaahs" than the entire Swedish National Pornographic Film Library') and ended, simply, by urging readers thus: 'You need to hear this album.'

The usually less excitable *Q* magazine gave Blur's debut album four-out-of-five stars, describing it as 'a substantially stocked treasure-chest of hit singles just waiting to happen'. And in *Vox*, another former *Sounds* journalist, Leo Finlay,

awarded 'Leisure' a whacking nine out of ten, acclaiming the 'range of styles and skills presented over the 12 tracks' and calling Blur 'the band of '91'.

Indie's bass supremo, Alex James

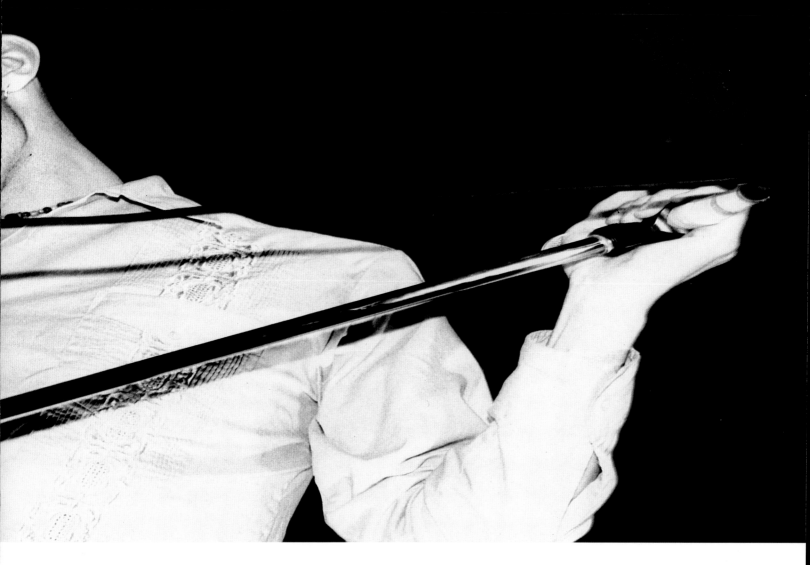

Then there were the 'quality' dailies. In the *Daily Telegraph*, former *NME* journalist Tony Parsons said Blur were 'the Stone Roses of Essex – and you can't rate anything much higher than that,' going on to describe the music on 'Leisure': 'It consists of fuzzy, ringing guitars, a pouting art school insouciance and dreamy songs that you can remember after hearing them once . . . "Leisure" has a freshness and infectious joy about it that I have not encountered since the Roses' one and only album.' And the *Guardian* critic wrote: '"Leisure" does the business well enough, being a tight little cluster of songs featuring nippy tunes and wilful layers of guitars.'

It seemed as though everyone was falling under Blur's spell.

NEGATIVE REACTIONS

ALMOST everyone, that is.

Thus far, the ratio of favourable to bad Blur reviews was running at approximately 99 to one. But now, the dreaded 'backlash' looked as though it might not be too far off as the band started getting some of their worst ever write-ups.

Now, it must be stressed that the music press does not deliberately build groups up just so that they can, just as deliberately, knock them down when they see fit. That is a myth, a lie. No, what happens is this: journalist discovers new band, writes enthusiastically about them for paper, tells fellow hacks about band, after which the keen ones proceed to pen their own paeans to this fabulous new discovery. Finally, after all the writers on the paper who like the band have had their say, the time comes for other voices to be heard.

Of course, some of these may be dissenting voices, but better that, surely, than blanket approval from an organ of the press that is supposed to offer balanced journalism and unbiased critiques? (Of course, some rock writers do fancy themselves as iconoclasts and would jump at the chance to topple any Emperors who have just been raised, fully decked out in New Clothes, on to a lofty pedestal.)

Dave Rowntree in Regular Geezer mode

Damon in his element – festival land

Anyway, some time around the release of 'Leisure' we got a glimpse of the dark side of this 'balanced journalism'. *Sky* magazine stayed on the fence about the record – 'It's quite good in a post-indie-house-cum-psychedelic-metal sort of way' – but *Siren* was more decisive, referring to Damon's 'poorly realised lyrical ideas'. The man from the *Independent* was equally unequivocal:

'Blur trudge rather than strut . . . guitars thrum desultorily, only arranging themselves into songs, it seems, by purest accident . . .

the general sluggishness extends to the lyrics, which congeal around a sense of dislocation and apathy . . . Listening to this album is the aural equivalent of deciding to become a heroin addict: choosing, over and over again, a state of stupefaction.'

There was more. 'Blur just sound bored,' reckoned *Making Music*. 'An uninspired group of dullards' whose conformity and conservatism will doubtless ensure them the celebrity they so desperately crave,' hissed London's *City Limits*, while, across the

Atlantic, *Spin* were downright nasty: 'This record really sucks. The Stone Roses were unlistenable schmaltz - who needs a dull carbon copy?

'"Leisure",' the American hack continued to spew forth bile, 'sounds so exhaustingly uninspired that you need 12 cups of espresso to stay awake during the entire thing. From the band's promo pic, it's evident that these Brits have spent more of their advance money on clothes and hair than on secondary matters such as rehearsal time . . . wretched music . . . bad juvenile pseudo-poetry . . . watered-down disco psychedelia . . .'

You get the idea.

Most worrying of all the slag-offs were the ones that appeared in the two surviving music weeklies, *NME* and *Melody Maker* – the two earliest, and most ardent champions, of the band. In his review of 'Leisure', the *NME*'s Andrew Collins digressed from his assessment of their musical worth to make a sideswipe at Blur's apparent lack of star quality.

'There is no mystique to Blur,' complained the obviously mystique-drenched journalist. 'They make Ride look like Duran Duran and they have taken Ordinary Ladness to new and frankly depressing extremes.'

Miaow.

It was left to *Melody Maker*'s Andrew Mueller to stick the boot in most savagely, however, in a review of Blur's admittedly lacklustre performance at that summer's Reading Festival.

'As breathlessly inspiring live experiences go, Blur are about as useful as a bootful of stale piss,' Mueller seethed. 'Bloodless nursery rhyme vocals mince about feebly against a backdrop of transparent guitars and shapeless tunes . . . All the songs sound like each other played at slightly different speeds . . . It has been written that Blur are "a celebration of youth". Bollocks to that: being young has nothing to do with being so lazy, so excited to be adequate, so bereft of fire, so tired.'

Oh dear.

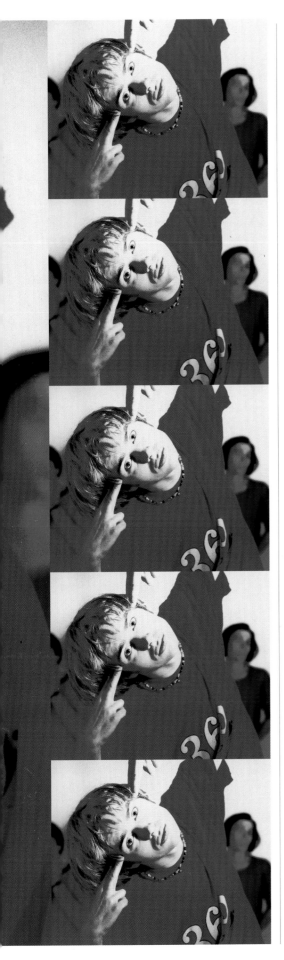

THE DOWNWARD SPIRAL

THE second half of 1991 wasn't all bad news for Blur. They did, after all, go Top 10 with their debut LP. They performed live to nine million listeners, and in front of 20,000 people, on Skegness beach for the *Radio 1 Roadshow*. They appeared on the marvellous *8.15 From Manchester* Saturday morning kiddie TV programme. They spent a day at the seaside with *Smash Hits*.

What's more, they entertained thousands of sweat-soaked revellers at the Reading Festival. And they even turned up alongside such glittering luminaries as Guns 'N Roses, Kenny Thomas, Page 3 Stunna Suzanne Mizzi and, um, World Of Twist (who?) to the self-styled party of the year –- 'Rave '– 'The bash to beat them all', set up by the *Daily Star*'s lovely Linda Duff.

yet another bunch of over-hyped limey guitar-slingers – with a set choc-full of swaggering rock'n'roll noise.

The *NME*'s Danny Kelly was there.

'They are simply magnificent,' Kelly glowed with British pride. 'And the kids go absolutely stark-raving bonkers. They understand this music (souped-up American R&B tinged with Sixties harmonies) and, whipped into a foaming froth by the demon Damon, they hurl themselves, like wave upon wave of rockhopper penguins, up on to the stage.'

This ecstatic American reaction to Blur was both pleasing and surprising: pleasing because it set up the band quite nicely for any future tours of the States, and surprising because, in spite of what Kelly wrote about the audience empathising with The Blur

The Soup Dragons – baggy's nadir

Blur didn't just spend the rest of 1991 being liggers with attitude, though. They also managed to add one incendiary live performance to their CV with their gig at New York's legendary Marquee club. By all accounts, Blur were astonishing that night, thrilling the assembled sceptics – who were expecting the usual crushing let-down from

Ethos, there is something very English about the group that one doesn't expect to be able to translate across the Atlantic.

Like Damon Albarn's heroes such as The Jam, The Smiths, The Kinks and Madness who failed to make any impact in America, Blur's music – and, in particular, Albarn's defiantly English enunciation – occasionally

veers towards that peculiar stereotype, Quintessential Britishness, one that, historically, has rarely excited mainstream American audiences.

Between October and December 1991, Blur dressed up as Blondie (with Damon as Debbie Harry!) for the *NME* Christmas issue, took their trousers off for TV presenter and DJ Gary Crowley, undertook yet another gruelling tour of Britain, played in France and performed alongside labelmates Jesus Jones, Diesel Park West, Sensitize and Whirlpool at the Food Christmas party at the Brixton Academy.

It was at the Brixton bash that the first 2,000 punters through the door were given a various artists cassette featuring a demo version of 'Resigned' (which would later appear on 1993's 'Modern Life Is Rubbish') as well as a new mix of the 'Leisure' track, 'High Cool'. In fact, the latter track was also distributed as a 12-inch promo single in a sharp gold-and-blue Food sleeve, specially designed for the occasion.

Food boss Andy Ross said at the time: 'We didn't want to put out another single just for the sake of it, so we did something that wasn't commercially available and didn't take the piss out of the fans.'

Reviews of Blur's performance at Brixton were complimentary enough ('"Bang" and "There's No Other Way" are as ace as they ever were,' said *Melody Maker*'s Sally Margaret Joy; 'An amplified snarl of punky energy and veiled threat,' frothed Stephen Dalton of Vox), and yet one still couldn't remove the vague sense of disappointment as Blur entered their third year, the vague sense that, despite the hit singles and concert appearances, this was a band who had yet to fully realise the promise of their first few months, and all the promises of their cover stories and rave reviews.

More than a vague sense of disappointment, it actually all felt like one

huge anti-climax, like the band had already gone as far as they could and that they just had some miserable future touting their tunes around Britain's scuzziest venues to look forward to.

This was as much the media's fault as it was the band's. It was the media, after all, who had made such grandiose claims for Blur. No wonder they had failed to live up to said claims, failed to go truly supernova, failed to become a world-beating act in their first 18 months. On the other hand, Blur had made a few (zillion) grandiose claims of their own, so maybe this was fate's cruel way of teaching them not to be so bloody full of themselves.

In the Christmas issue of *Melody Maker*, a short piece by Steve Sutherland looking back on Blur's year summed up this feeling of comedown: 'They had the look, they had the sound, and 1991 should have been theirs. But it wasn't, it was Bryan Adams', and it may well be that even the estimable Damon Albarn won't be able to talk Blur into any other place in history than that of one-hit-wonders.'

The trouble was the sheer size of Blur's ambitions. 'The scale we're working on is so enormous,' they told *Select* in October '91. 'We're trying to reach absolutely everybody. The whole world . . .' Blur had established total world domination as their entire raison d'être from the offset. When they failed to be The Biggest Band In The Cosmos by the end of 1991, what else could we all do but feel the teensiest bit let down?

There was another element contributing to Blur's ever-so-slightly declining fortunes, one completely out of their control: the Fickle Factor. Not just the British music press, but British pop audiences in general, are notoriously capricious. A year is a long time in pop. So, whereas at the start of 1991 Blur looked like the brightest, brashest burst of brilliance to emerge since the last bright, brash burst of brilliance, by the end of the year there was something tired about them and their sound.

Remember, this was a look and sound bound up in the 'Madchester'/'baggy' scene of the early Nineties and great groups like The Stone Roses and Happy Mondays. By late '91, however, 'baggy' was a term of derision, one usually flung at sub-Roses copyists like The Bridewell Taxis, Northside, The Soup Dragons, The Farm, The High, Inspiral Carpets, Sensitize and The Mock Turtles whose lethargic, listless rhythms, gurning, gormless expressions and Ecstasy-warped brains made a complete mockery of the Roses-cum-Mondays immaculate indie dance floor ethic.

The world, one sensed, was waiting for something dazzlingly new to ignite the nation's airwaves, something to blow the blasted 'baggy' away. Horribly enough, it occurred that maybe Blur had a bit of a naff baggy look themselves, what with their sloppy, loose-fitting, collarless shirts, multi-coloured beads, floppy page-boy fringes and all.

Worse still, it occurred that maybe the band once described as 'the Bros of baggy' had a – whisper it – generic baggy sound, what with the slow-mo rhythms of 'She's So High', 'High Cool' and the rest. While Blur still had a considerable following and would regularly draw hundreds, even thousands, to their gigs, one couldn't get rid of the nagging feeling that they had reached their peak, reached an impasse.

Ironically, in the October '91 issue of *Select*, Damon announced to David Cavanagh that 'Leisure' wasn't part of the problem – the symptom, as it were, of pop's current malaise – it was the cure.

'The next album will be the start of a new era,' Albarn declared, as confident as ever. 'This one's been the death of the blank, directionless era we've just been through. This one is the "Kill Baggy" album. Well, we've done that now. We've killed baggy.'

For the first time, however, there was something hollow, something unconvincing about Damon's brave declaration of intent.

Damon: a well-read *and* a well-dressed man

Graham Coxon, pretending to tune up

★★★★☆☆☆☆★★★★

Dark Life

THE BRETT-ISH EMPIRE

IF there was a vague feeling about Blur that they were Last Year's Models, it was heightened by the arrival of glittering new indie princelings Suede who, in early 1992, were featured on the cover of *Melody Maker* with the now endlessly regurgitated headline, 'The Best New Band In Britain'. This was before Suede even had a record out, and it mirrored the way *Sounds* bravely put Blur on the cover long before the release of their first single.

> ewcomers Suede threaten to eclipse Blur altogether ... the band's growing reputation for drunkenness gets worse ... their 'Popscene' single fails to set world alight ... 'Rollercoaster' tour with Mary Chain, Valentines and Dinosaur Jr ... bad experiences in America ... the band face financial problems, musical difficulties, critical disdain, public disinterest and are threatened with dismissal the from their record company ...

As *Record Collector* recalls: 'Events in Britain were overtaking Blur fast, and it was clear that a new, post-baggy order was beginning to emerge, quite possibly with the dashing Suede as its elite guard.'

For Damon Albarn, the thought that Suede might one day soon usurp Blur's position as British indiepop's reigning champions was even more unbearable because his new girlfriend, Justine Frischmann (who currently leads the highly promising four-piece punk-pop band, Elastica), used to step out with Suede frontman Brett Anderson. Worse still in this burgeoning soap opera-style hate-triangle, Justine used to be Suede's rhythm guitarist! It is claimed by some that la Frischmann even thought of Suede's name . . .

Not surprisingly, the rivalry between Damon and Brett got, at times, pretty intense. Matters were exacerbated by Bernard Butler (the Suede guitarist who left the band in summer 1994) who, in the *NME*, took it upon himself to choose some lines from Blur's 'Bang' ('Bang goes another day/Where it went I cannot say') as the worse lyrics he had ever heard in his life.

It wasn't long, therefore, before veiled references to Suede started to appear in Blur articles. The first ones were at least reasonably diplomatic, Damon usually opting to refer to Suede as 'the "S" word'.

Then there was the time Damon went a bit further and said: 'I don't think you'd have Suede without Blur. Well, I know you wouldn't.' Or the time he was asked to proffer comments on his 'successors' and, choosing his words very carefully, said: 'It's very difficult for me to have a straightforward opinion of Suede because there's so much fundamental rivalry between the two of us.'

However, in an interview with *Select*, Alex James was less restrained, and he just seemed to snap.

'Borrowed money. Borrowed talent. Borrowed quotes. Borrowed time . . . at a good rate of interest,' said the coolly caustic bass guitarist of the pretenders to the Britpop throne.

It wasn't just churlishness or personal vendettas on Blur's part that made them feel enmity towards Suede –- this was a professional matter. Blur reckoned Suede's immaculate English pop, and Brett Anderson's mock Cockney Rebel vocal mannerisms, were pretty much their own inventions, and that Suede were getting credit for something Blur created themselves. Plus, because Suede were new and Blur had been around (in pop terms) for yonks, the former were having success after success while Blur, simply, weren't.

'All it boils down to in the end is that Suede had a really good year last year and we had a really bad year,' Damon calmly reflected in *Sky* magazine 12 months later, although he did summon up sufficient animosity to refer to something an acquaintance of his had said with regard to Brett's rear end: 'A friend of mine wondered how anyone could think of Brett Anderson as a sex symbol when he's got such a big arse.'

Ouch.

SHELTER SKELTER

SHOWDOWN time. Suede and Blur met face to face in early 1992 at *NME*'s Gimme Shelter Party, a live extravaganza at London's Town & Country Club designed to raise money for homeless people, and you could virtually see and hear the lines – the one on the rise, the other on the decline – intersecting with a bang on pop's giant graph paper.

By most accounts, Suede – third on the bill – were terrific while headliners Blur were awful that night, getting pissed up before the gig and playing abysmally during it.

'They were in a state of such extraordinary drunkenness it was a small miracle they could stand, let alone perform,' recalled The Stud Brothers in *Melody Maker* some time later, echoing Damon's own comments in *Sky* magazine: 'We were drinking so much we could hardly play our instruments.'

The reviews of 'Gimme Shelter' were cruel yet, in restrospect, the venom spat in Blur's direction was probably fairly deserved.

'They're the English version of LA rock bands,' said the man from *MM*, fed up with Blur's infantile antics, 'bored rich kids smashing their way through executive allowances. Damon pretends his mic is a dick. Damon hits his head against the speaker. Damon is a prat.'

The *NME* hack was so scathing about Blur's performance that night ('Carry On Punk Rock,' he called it) that the paper's Editor felt compelled to add a semi-apology at the bottom of the review.

Damon Albarn himself didn't help

Suede, Blur's arch-rivals, in 1993

matters, prefacing Blur's erratic performance with the immortal introduction: 'We're so fucking shit, you may as well go home now.'

A year later, Damon looked back on that night with regret.

'It was a terrible gig – the girls at the front were almost in tears when they saw just how debauched these *Smash Hits* idols had become.

'The thing was,' he continued, 'it was supposed to be our comeback.

'But, at that time, we felt that there was no way any journalist was going to give us a break if we played with someone like Suede,' the singer went on to explain to John Harris. 'We had nothing to focus on - no new records, primarily - and we felt like massive underdogs. We just got really drunk and didn't play at all well. That was the point at which we realised that we were becoming slightly schizophrenic, that we weren't thinking straight.'

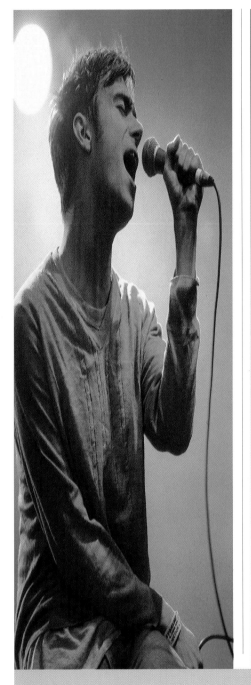

Three faces of Damon Albarn

SHOOTING 'STARSHAPED'

IT was around this time that Blur's drinking, always something of a hobby, became something of a problem.

A review in the *NME* of a Blur gig at some dive in south London in early 1992 made plain the band's dilemma.

'"Excuse me," barks a confused, teenage voice beside me. "Do you know who this is?" Oh, how soon the kids forget,' lamented the writer, long-term Blur aficionado Gina Morris, adding: 'Every time I've seen Blur over the past year they've been tanked up and fucked off.'

For grim documentary evidence of their infatuation with the bottle at that time, one needs to look no further than Blur's 'Starshaped' video, an astonishingly frank and fearless – or, depending on your vantage point, crass and stupid – account of a group of musicians literally on the verge of collective mental collapse.

'At this point, I thought I was going mad,' Graham Coxon told *Indicator*, around the same time he was advised by his doctor to lay off alcohol for six months – or else be forced to face the consequences. 'I thought I was having a nervous breakdown.'

If you can stomach it, 'Starshaped' makes for incredibly compelling viewing, featuring as it does shot after shot of various band members in the unpleasant throes of hangover dementia, all squiffy, bloodshot

Blur in their 'tired and emotional' phase

eyes and booze-blanched/puffed faces, feeling tired and emotional and/or slumped miserably across tables in repulsive motorway cafes.

There is one particularly memorable scene where drummer Dave Rowntree – the sensible one, remember, the one likened to 'a thoughtful squaddie' – dives semi-naked into a freezing cold river with just a can of Heineken in his hand to keep his skinny white frame warm.

Then there are the numerous sadistic close-ups of Messrs Albarn and Coxon vomiting fountainfuls of bile hither and, more often than not, thither: shooting puke through their nostrils, pouring it out their mouths all over the floor or even, in one obscenely graphic instance, all over their shoes – all in glorious technicolour.

One 'Starshaped' scene grabs the attention, only for different reasons. It may be less stomach-churning than the others, but it is no less affecting and it was filmed some time in early 1993. It starkly but neatly sums up Blur's terrible year. There they all

'Ere, Dave, d'you think we look daft holding these daffs?'

sit, around the table of yet another hideous service station greasy spoon. Suddenly, a bleary-eyed Damon turns towards the camera and repeats the question asked by the off-camera interviewer.

'What was it like in Blur in 1992?'

Then silence. Nothing. Just four blank expressions and much humming and hawing and embarrassed staring into space. Because even Blur couldn't force themselves to contrive one of their trademark, jolly, absurdist responses to this most painful of enquiries, one that brought back so many unpleasant memories of their 12 darkest months. It is a truly poignant moment.

'POPSCENE' BUT NOT HEARD

THEN they released their fourth single, 'Popscene', and things went from bad to worse. The problem wasn't that 'Popscene', released in March 1992, was a duff record.

Far from it. In fact, with its speed-fuelled melody and brash, blazing horns it sounded like The Teardrop Explodes' 'Reward' played by The Sex Pistols – a Good Thing, indeed. Its extra tracks were pretty impressive as well, marking a change in musical direction for the band with the punky pugnacity of 'I'm Fine', the New Wave neurosis of 'Mace' and swirling rifferama of 'Garden Central'.

No, more than the lukewarm critical reaction to the single, the problem really lay in the failure of 'Popscene' to connect in a big enough way with the general public. Considering that this was Blur's first single for almost a year, the fact that it only reached the Number 32 slot was extremely disappointing for a band who always set so much store by commercial success.

Blur's label boss Andy Ross remembers well how upset everyone in the Blur camp felt at this juncture.

Johnny Lydon – *ne* Rotten . . .

'Just keep smiling, Alex, and no one'll notice'

... with the Sex Pistols at their punkiest

'We were totally devastated,' he says. 'We were in a state of shock for months. We couldn't believe it, because we all thought "Popscene" was such a brilliant song.'

It probably wouldn't be overly dramatic to say the failure of 'Popscene' plunged the entire Blur contingent into a deep crisis of confidence. Damon recalls the sense of ignominious defeat that surrounded the band during this difficult period.

'We felt that "Popscene" was a big departure, a very, very English record, but that annoyed a lot of people. And because fashion was completely myopic about America at the time – the only bands people really cared about were Nirvana and Pearl Jam – we felt that we were being mistreated,' he says, referring to the near-hegemony of the music scene by the so-called grunge bands from the States. 'We knew that record was good, we knew it was better than what we'd done before, but certain reviewers hated us for it. We put ourselves out on a limb to pursue this English ideal, and no one was interested.'

How much worse could things get?

COAST TO 'ROLLERCOASTER'

QUITE a bit, actually.

In April '92, Blur undertook the 'Rollercoaster' package tour of Britain – it was set up as Blighty's response to America's mighty, annual 'Lollapalooza' travelling circus – alongside Dinosaur Jr, My Bloody Valentine and The Jesus & Mary Chain, and in truth, it really did them no favours whatsoever.

To be honest, Blur seemed out of their depth next to these pioneers of avant-rock noise. They were dwarfed by My Bloody Valentine's towering experiments, were made to sound slight in comparison to

Dinosaur's tidal waves of grungy guitar, and were made to look like kindergarten miscreants next to the radical delinquency of the Mary Chain.

'Their tuneful if truculent pop came across at half-kilter,' said the *Guardian*. 'The impassioned flailing of their new single "Popscene" came across like The Jam at their least disciplined, suggesting that the gamey psychedelia of Blur's records may already have run its course.'

The *Melody Maker*'s David Stubbs was less kind-spirited. He was particularly unimpressed by Blur's new, noisy direction.

'Their newfound feedback is deployed as if squirted from a water pistol,' wrote Herr Stubbs. 'They look like the Grange Hill School band and they spend the evening attempting to divert attention from their stinted, underwrought, ordinary sound by various means – Damon wears an atrocious jumper, pulls out a megaphone, even at one truly sad point pulls down his trousers and underwear and leaps about the stage like a man whose bogroll has slipped under the trap door.'

The *Melody Maker*'s Stud Brothers were just about the only journalists on the planet with a kind word to say about Blur at this point. First they praised 'Popscene' – 'It's light years away from the ambient abstractions that came to define The Scene That Celebrates Itself. It's a Nineties punk rock song with a horn-driven biker chorus and heavy doses of narcissism and nihilism courtesy of Damon – then they raved about 'Rollercoaster', calling it 'the best show you'll see this year'.

Damon himself – enlivened by the concurrent interest in the band of former Pink Floyd visual effects man, the legendary Storm Thorgeson who saw many similarities between Blur and Syd Barrett-era Floyd and was keen to make a film with them – was equally excited about the four-bands-in-a-row show, describing it as 'the best thing that's happened to British music in a long time'.

'I'm a bit starstruck by it all,' he commented about his temporary tourmates and idols, 'but I'm delighted that we're going to be playing with them.'

Damon discovers mod fashion at least two years before it's back in vogue

But really, even Albarn's irrepressible energy, boundless enthusiasm and inexhaustible optimism was taxed to the max by the next instalment in Blur's Blue Period.

AMERICA, THE . . . UGLY

THERE were a couple of brief respites in this, easily Blur's most relentlessly awful year to date. They played a rousing set at Fulham's Hibernian Club, supported by that season's leading Situationist-style punk-pop activists, the so-called 'Riot Grrrls' known as Huggy Bear. It was at this gig that the band gave away a one-sided seven-inch single, the truly bizarre 'The Wassailing Song'.

And then in spring 1992, the band visited Japan for a series of concerts and found themselves on the receiving end of the sort of rapturous devotion not witnessed since the headiest days of Beatlemania. But even the feverish response of thousands of adoring Japanese teenies didn't really console the band.

'The tour in Japan went really well,' Damon told *Sky* magazine, 'but – and I don't want to sound horrible here – all you need to get mobbed in Japan is to have blond hair and be more than five feet tall. Being mobbed,' he added, 'is so . . . unrefined.'

Then, in the summer of 1992, Blur undertook a 44-date tour of America, forced by their record company to break the place state by state and encouraged by the warm reception they got in New York the previous November. This jaunt, however, was rather less successful. Or, as *Record Collector* puts it, 'It quickly became a half-hearted, drunken series of disasters.'

America was definitely less keen to capitulate this time round. As The Stud Brothers said of this completely disastrous venture: 'The Yanks just didn't understand why Blur were neither EMF [the noisébeat boys from the West Country whose infectious indie-dance single, "Unbelievable", had been Number One in the States the previous summer] nor Happy Mondays, and Blur themselves began to feel that, unless they found a reason for being in a group pretty bloody sharpish, there wouldn't be a group at all.'

'Oi, you at the back there, stop that talking !'

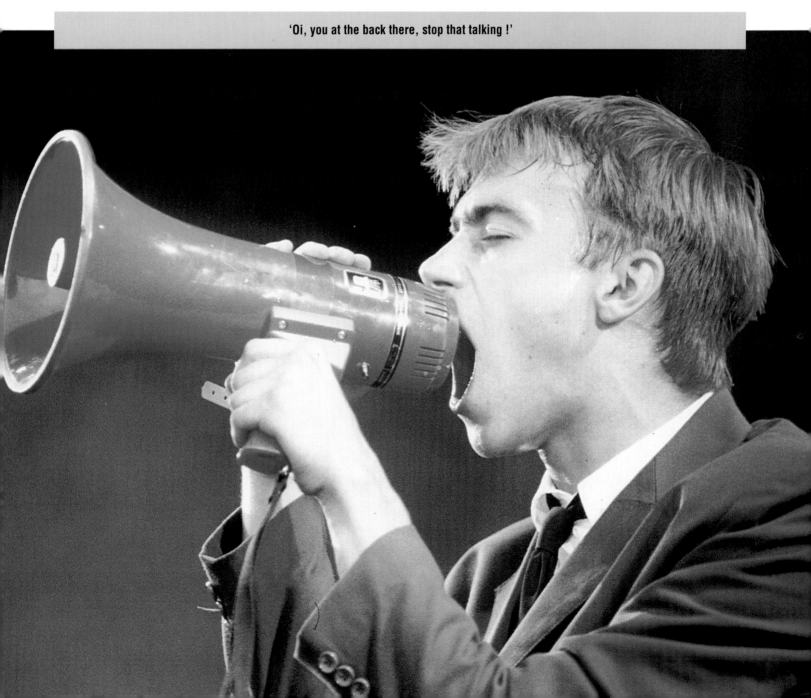

Matters were made worse by the group's increasing feelings of unease at being in America at all.

'I get physically ill when I go there,' claimed Damon, while, in *Select*, David Cavanagh detailed Blur's disgust with the country and its 'ceaseless tableau of malls and bubble culture'.

Damon recalls the trip with less than relish: 'We were shellshocked. The whole thing was just a terrible experience. The drinking got really bad, for a start. Problem was, we had to go there for two months, out of which we had three days off.

'We did 44 dates, and each one seemed to involve getting off the bus and being greeted by a record company rep who'd put us in a big, black car and drive us to shopping malls where we'd have to "meet and greet", eat shit in a fast food store and then go to a radio station where they'd think we were from Manchester. Actually playing onstage was the only release we got from the constant irritation, and we just became completely exhausted.'

Completely homesick, too: 'I just started to miss really simple things,' Damon says. 'I missed people queuing up in shops. I missed people saying "goodnight" on the BBC. I missed having 15 minutes between commercial breaks. And I missed people having respect for my geographical roots, because Americans don't care if you're from Inverness or Land's End. I missed everything about England.'

The band's first American gig of the tour, at Boston's Venus De Milo, was a total nightmare, as Max Bell of *Vox* relates.

'Over-fortified by a brace of Jagermeister, Blur found themselves in a full-scale riot featuring every rock'n'roll cliché in the book: promoter switches power off, audience destroys hall, band assaults bouncers, who chase band into broom cupboard, band escape via window to waiting car, run into blood-soaked fans, and so on.'

'We were at rock bottom,' admits Alex James, 'utterly frustrated. Our relationships with each other were awful, we were practically hospital cases.'

Meanwhile, back in the UK, and to add insult to injury, there were a couple of disasters. First, there was a production balls-up when sessions for their next album, which was meant to be produced by XTC's Andy Partridge (whose studio demeanour, according to the *NME*'s John Harris, was akin to that of a strict headmaster), were mysteriously shelved. (The Partridge mixes of 'Seven Days', 'Coping' and 'Sunday Sunday' have yet to see the light of day, as has a cover of the Buggles' bubblegum hit from 1979, 'Video Killed The Radio Star'.)

If this wasn't bad enough, a financial balls-up of near-catastrophic proportions awaited them at home: Blur found out one day while they were away that all their royalties for 'Leisure' had gone walkies.

'While we were in the States,' Damon shudders at the memory, 'we discovered that all the money we'd made from "Leisure" – which wasn't millions, but quite a reasonable amount, nonetheless – had "disappeared". We'd worked as hard as people like Ride or The Charlatans, but we hadn't seen anything. We literally had no money; we couldn't even pay our rent, and it got to the stage where it was touch and go whether or not we'd go bankrupt.'

This dreadful state of affairs led Blur to split from their management company and, with their financial/musical fortunes at an all-time low and beer-guzzling at an all-time high, their record company, Food – who thus far had been so supportive – gave the band an ultimatum: pull yourself together or be dropped from the label.

★★★★★ ★ ★★★★★ ★★★★

Mod Life

Blur reinvent themselves brilliantly with sharp neo-Mod look ... 'For Tomorrow' single is best yet ... Dave gets into fight with a Buzzcock ... Damon explains why modern life is rubbish just in time for the release of second LP 'Modern Life Is Rubbish' ... critical and commercial tides turn once more in favour of Blur ... Blur almost get into hot bother with their anti-US attitude and assertion that British culture 'is under siege' ... 'Sugary Tea' tour ... after killing baggy, Blur kill grunge ...

THE BRIT PACK

WHAT Blur needed was to tear up the plans and start all over again. What they needed, basically, was to find a brand new look, concept and sound. (They also needed new management, which they got when, at the 11th hour, Mary Chain/Midge Ure manager Chris Morrison intervened to save Blur's skin.) What they needed, in short, was to drastically reinvent themselves.

They did it.

Now, anyone who saw Blur hanging around the backstage area down at Reading in summer '92 would already have been familiar with Damon Albarn's natty grey suit and the other chaps' mod-ish togs.

But the Blur who blew us away in spring 1993 was something else entirely. This was the band taking their obsession with the sharp Carnaby Street-style threads of the mid-Sixties to its logical conclusion. This, to give their new look its full glorious self-penned monicker, was 'British Image Number 1'.

There they were in the news pages of *Melody Maker* and the *NME*, hands arrogantly-but-casually placed in pockets, leaning against a dirty white wall – daubed on which, in true yob-graffiti scrawl, was the aforementioned slogan 'British Image Number 1' – all neatly cropped haircuts, three-quarter-length Levis, Doc Martens, mod blazers and Fred Perrys. And the finishing touch? That ubiquitous, menacing working man's plaything, the Great Dane.

Aware of the connotations of such a look, Damon was quick to deny flirting with skinhead, fascist imagery, and he assured *NME* readers that what they saw was not necessarily what they were going to get. 'This is not a nationalistic thing,' he said.

Call it nationalistic, call it Anglophile, call it post-modern ultra-mod, call it what you liked, the Blur boys had radically altered their appearance from shaggable, soft-focus indie-pups to hyperreal hard-men facing the fin-de-siècle future in functional streetwear.

Whatever, in this, the fifth year of their existence, Blur looked like a completely brand new band.

'TOMORROW' PEOPLE

AND they sounded like one, too.

Suitably jolted into direct action by threats from their record company (see the end of chapter four), Blur entered the studio in late autumn '92 with producer Stephen Street, who started bashing their fresh material into delicious pop shapes. The recording sessions went well, and by early 1993, they nearly had enough tracks for that perennially tricky Difficult Second Album.

However, there was still something missing: a hit single.

Cue 'For Tomorrow'.

'For Tomorrow', released in April 1993, was Blur's first truly great record. You could almost say it was worth the four-year wait. It featured a weird, 'phased', Seventies production sound that recalled Tony Visconti's work with David Bowie, a vocal that harked back to 'Laughing Gnome'-era Bowie, and showcased a Damon Albarn lyric that suggested he was finally getting to grips with his half-inched Jean Paul Sartre-esque theory about the modern world being disorientating and 'nauseating' ('He's a 20th Century boy/With his hands on the rails/Trying not to be sick again/And holding on for tomorrow,' went the words).

'For Tomorrow' was classic pop music in excelsis: at once calculated and cretinous, it may have been clever and complex, yet it retained that all-important common touch – specifically, a musical hook you could hang your coat on, a ludicrously hummable chorus and a series of la-la-la-la-las that, somehow, managed to be more infectious than embarrassing.

Blur, ever-prolific and ever-generous, tossed away six extra tracks on the flipside of the various formats of 'For Tomorrow', although, on reflection, they really shouldn't have bothered.

With the 12-inch you got 'Into Another' (bog-standard swirly psychedelia) and 'Hanging Over' (yet more bog-standard swirly psychedelia); with part one of the two-CD set, you got 'Peach', a strange, slow Syd Barrett-ish curio about holes in heads and birds' nests (but no mentions of

SIXTY

Is it Damon? Is it David ?

Blur: chairmen of the (key) board

Alex and Dave in rare reflective mood

peaches), and the similarly spacey 'Bone Bag'; and with part two, there was the 'Sgt Pepper'-like, music hall oompah trombone jauntiness of 'When The Cows Come Home' as well as the (yawn) bog-standard swirly psychedelia of 'Beachcoma', not forgetting an acoustic version of 'For Tomorrow', which proved that Blur didn't need any new-fangled studio gadgetry or state-of-the-art recording techniques to tart up their basically robust material.

OUTRAGE HARD

'FOR Tomorrow', with its lovely sleeve painting of World War Two fighter bombers, zoomed into the charts at Number 28 in May 1993. Not only that but the critics loved it as well. The *NME* referred to it as 'a pop outrage the likes of which Blur have never hinted at before' and praised its sonic similarity to the work of ELO. (A compliment, apparently.) Meanwhile, *What's On* called it 'a magnificent single that bristles with off-the-wall melodies and evil undercurrents of social destruction', whatever that meant.

To celebrate their critical/commercial victory – a double whammy if ever there was one – 'Uncle' Dave Rowntree got into a fight with Tony Barber of The Buzzcocks at the launch party for the latter's 'Trade Test Transmissions' comeback LP. The *Daily Star* of April 26th reported the fracas in fine style.

'Top Of The Bops', read the superb headline, while the rather less hysterical sub-heading went: 'Exclusive On The Battle Of The Bands'. And the story itself was no less entertaining.

'Traffic in London's Soho was brought to a standstill as the rebel stars slugged it out in the street. There were hits all round. The odds looked good for Blur as their tall, thin 25-year-old drummer squared up to the spiky-haired thirtysomething Buzzcock.

'POW! Punk rocker Tony launched a barrage of blows on the Blur drummer's face.

'THUD! Dave fought back with an uppercut that Frank Bruno would have been proud of.

'SMASH! The brawlers brought traffic to a halt as their fight spilled onto the packed West End streets.

'WALLOP! Sexy singer Miki from Lush jumped in to stop the fisticuffs.

'CRASH! Pie-eyed Dave sulked off home with a black eye.

'CRUNCH! Punch-drunk Tony was carted off to the cells after police spotted him arguing with onlookers.'

Someone described at the end of the *Star*'s report as 'an embarrassed Blur spokesman' neatly explained away the incident, saying it was 'just high spirits that got out of hand'.

A bit like the incident, around the same time, involving Blur, a blank seaside wall and a can of spraypaint. So pleased were the band with their second great zeitgeist-capturing slogan of the year – Modern Life Is

Association demanded that the miscreants should be 'made to come back and repaint the whole building – and the money for materials should come from their album royalties'. Local Lib-Dem councillor Mike Bargent slammed the band's behaviour ('Totally irresponsible') while concerned Conservative Audrey Overton described it as 'pure vandalism'.

It was like punk actually happened.

'Jim stops and gets out the car, goes to a house in Emperor's Gate, through the door and to his room, then he puts the TV on, turns it off and makes some tea, says Modern Life Is Rubbish . . .'

Then news stories in the weekly music papers started appearing about Blur's long-awaited follow-up to 'Leisure' which was to be titled, suggestively enough, 'Modern Life Is Rubbish'. There was obviously a Very

Graham and Damon teach the New Wave of New Wave whippersnappers all about Punk! Rock! Energy!

Rubbish – that they decided to paint it big and black all along the side of the newly-redecorated Clacton Bandstand Pavilion during a photo session for the *NME*.

According to the local newspaper, the *Colchester Gazette*, the chairman of the Clacton Hoteliers And Guest House

ON A 'RUBBISH' TIP
OUR first glimpse of the band's provocative new phrase, 'Modern Life Is Rubbish', had been on the inner sleeve of 'For Tomorrow', where the lyrics, clearly printed, featured a cryptic spoken outro by Albarn that included the lines:

Serious Cultural Point being made here. Damon explained what the title meant in an interview with the *NME*.

'Modern life is the rubbish of the past,' he said. 'Rubbish in the sense of a collection of debris from the past. We all live on the rubbish: it dictates our thoughts. And

because it's all built up over such a long time, there's no necessity for originality anymore. There are so many old things to splice together in infinite permutations that there is absolutely no need to create anything new.

'I think,' he finished with a flourish, and you could sense Albarn was building up to a gigantically immodest statement here, 'that phrase is the most significant comment on popular culture since "Anarchy In The UK". That's why I want to graffiti it everywhere. I think it expresses everything.'

As get-out clauses go, this ranked with the best. What Damon Albarn had (brilliantly) managed to do in these few sentences was provide him and his band with the perfect excuse for any accusations of derivativeness or retro-mongering that were likely to be hurled in Blur's direction on the release of their second album. If and when critics suggested 'Modern Life Is Rubbish' was merely a clever pastiche of past sounds and styles, all Damon had to do was say, 'Ah, but that's the whole point of the record – it's a deliberate statement about the unoriginal nature of contemporary music and art' and he would be vindicated. 'Modern Life Is Rubbish' contained its very own in-built critique. Blur, the clever bastards, were now beyond reproach.

As it turned out, 'Modern Life Is Rubbish' was derivative in places, but it didn't matter because it was so smart, so sharp, so fine – Blur had learned to put their influences to good use at last. So, while there were echoes from the Sixties (The Kinks, Pink Floyd), the Seventies (The Jam, The Buzzcocks – oh, irony!) and the Eighties (Teardrop Explodes, Madness), the album was polished off with a Nineties, post-modern sheen that lent it a precise, contemporary feel.

'Modern Life Is Rubbish' was – still is, in fact! – a seriously diverse record, ranging from eerie modern blues ('Miss America') to art-punk ('Advert') to the poppily anthemic ('Starshaped') to melodic ballads ('Blue Jeans') to glam-rock ('Chemical World') to sardonic, knees-up party-time celebrations

('Sunday Sunday') to the melancholy synthesiser noodles of 'Resigned'.

However, unlike the messily eclectic 'Leisure', it all hung together superbly, sounding to all intents and purposes like a concept album - although with none of the dreaded Seventies prog-rock connotations of the word. And the concept was this: a journey around Nineties Britain, in and out of its suburbs where people sit gawping at sanitised TV shows and crap adverts for products they don't want, or perform formation car washing routines (see 'Sunday Sunday'); through anaesthetising shopping malls and plastic theme parks; up into the dirty urban streets and down into the suffocating environs of the London Underground tube system.

'You're introduced to a range of people and places, to rituals and relationships, that you end up empathising with, without ever having actually experienced,' wrote Paul Mathur in his *Melody Maker* review of the album. 'I've never been to "Villa Rosie" and I've quite possibly missed out on the delights of swallowing "Oily Water", but before too long I know exactly what Blur are on about.'

Damon echoed Mathur's sentiments when he said: 'We wanted to write something like an Essex version of Dylan Thomas' "Under Milk Wood". Something with a very definite sense of place, populated by very definite characters, and which would try to encapsulate modern England – on the one hand a romantic image, and on the other faintly sinister.'

'SIEGE' MENTALITY

THERE was a certain crusading zeal about 'Modern Life Is Rubbish' in particular and Blur in general during 1993. Evidently, the band were on something of a mission: they were standing FOR something – British life in all its multi-faceted, polycultural glory – and reacting AGAINST something else – the perceived colonisation (or, as *Melody Maker*'s Stud Brothers put it, the 'Coca-colonisation') of British culture by America and the way, as the above writers put it, 'the

Would you buy a pop single from these men?

Dylan Thomas, a key influence

Post-modern Piccadilly palaver

British have become increasingly estranged from their national environment, its mythologies and iconographies.'

Damon Albarn was only too keen to elucidate (some might cruelly say 'pontificate') on these and many other

matters to journalists at the time. In particular, he wanted to stem the wave of US guitar bands – whose lazy slacker ethos and pre-packaged, MTV-endorsed, sanitised rebellion he so abhorred – currently swamping the airwaves and the music press.

'If punk was about getting rid of hippies, then I'm getting rid of grunge,' Damon proudly announced in the *NME*. 'There's the same sort of feeling around today: people should smarten up a bit, be a bit more energetic. They're walking around like

The band pay homage to Noel Coward

hippies again – they're stooped, they've got greasy hair, there's no difference. Whether they like it or not, they're listening to Black Sabbath again. It irritates me.

'This album,' he added, 'doesn't just celebrate England, it's about the sinister Americanisation of this country.'

Alex James explained how much of the material for 'Modern Life Is Rubbish', which was, at one point, going to be called 'England Versus America', was written during the band's sojourn in the States.

'America made us realise what a wonderfully quiet, undramatic place Britain is,' said the bass player. 'We wrote virtually all the songs while we were out there. And when we came back we realised how much we like being British. The trouble is, when you start giving out those signals everyone thinks you're a fascist. You are not allowed to be British. You are not allowed to be German. But you are, of course, always allowed to be American.'

Albarn was more explicit in a now-famous *Melody Maker* issue devoted to celebrating British pop in all its myriad forms (black, white, whatever), one entitled 'Our Culture Is Under Siege' (itself part of a quotation lifted during the interview with Damon) and, perhaps insensitively when viewed in retrospect, subtitled 'The Empire Strikes Back'.

First, he lambasted America's mall culture: 'Life for Americans exists within these huge sheds,' he said, 'and you can eat and buy your shoes, listen to music and buy your health insurance, almost go to the hospital, in them . . . Americans are lobotomised, sanitised automatons.'

Then, homing in on the increasingly synthetic-looking pubs and bars that litter our high streets, he expanded on his theme: 'Britain's become a holiday camp full of cutesy, ordinary British people, all bobbing about like minnows in a heated pool. It's like pubs have become plastic replicas of what they once actually were; people have indulged in the wilful destruction of something and replaced it with a superficial version of what is was anyway.

'It's not as if it's some kind of modernist vision where they're trying to create a better world for everyone, it's like they're pandering to a certain idea that other people, particularly Americans,' he said, spitting out the last word like it was poison on his tongue, 'have of what Britain should be like. I'm not saying everyone should put on a fake Cockney accent and start singing about the Old Bull & Bush, but I do feel that our culture is under siege . . .'

These last five words, uttered, with unfortunate synchronicity, in exactly the same week that British National Party candidate Derek Beackon was elected as a local councillor in London's Tower Hamlets, created one hell of a stink at the time. It caused an unholy row among *MM* readers

He's in the Army now!

and unleashed a torrent of furious missives towards the *'Maker*'s letters page from those who took Albarn's admittedly provocative line out of context, added it to the band's new image – the regular streetwear of your average BNP follower – and saw red.

This was, of course, the very same year that Morrissey was metaphorically hung, drawn and quartered for draping his body in a Union Jack at his concert in London's Finsbury Park – the former Smiths frontman has yet to convince many people that he wasn't deliberately flirting with fascist

imagery and attracting The Wrong Sort Of Crowd. Perhaps fearful of the same sort of reaction, Blur were quick to nip any such accusations in the bud in the above *Melody Maker* interview.

'There's no suggestion whatsoever in anything we've ever done that we glorify a white Britain,' said Damon, firmly. 'In fact, what we're doing is celebrating Britain today, which is most definitely not white. Besides, to attract that kind of audience [ie, fascist thugs], we'd have to be more yobbish, and we're just too art school, too camp.

'TEA FOR TWO . . . THOUSAND

TOO true. Blur shamelessly flaunted their camp credentials on their 'Sugary Tea' tour of Great Britain throughout autumn '93, a tour part sponsored and co-promoted by *Melody Maker*.

With a stage set consisting of a giant sofa, a giant television, a giant greasy old cooker, a giant fridge and some giant table lamps – the whole thing looking like a grotesquely enormous front room from some Fifties suburban family dream (nightmare?) home – 'Sugary Tea' was the kitschily cartoon product of four quite vivid (and diseased?) imaginations.

Thousands of fans flocked to witness 'Sugary Tea''s humorous representation of the past and bizarre vision of the future. So, it seemed, did thousands of journalists who were eager to eat their earlier words about Blur being all washed up.

'The most contemporary of bitter pleasures,' concluded the *Melody Maker*. 'Blur have found strength through change,' declared the *NME*. 'Not one of your throwaway pop nights,' decided an unusually magnanimous *Time Out*. There was also a reference by one over-excitable pop writer to an as-yet-unrecorded song which appeared to display certain (dare we say it?) disco-ish tendencies – about which, more later . . .

Blur live, 1993

There were also thousands of people desperate to meet the band at the 'Sugary Tea Debates', which were specially set up by *Melody Maker* to take place before each gig and involved the four members of Blur sitting on a podium in the venue and facing a series of enquiries on a variety of topics (racism, sexism, our soundbite culture, Morrissey, the meaning of life . . .) from fans – Damon, Graham, Alex and Dave looked for all the world like the panel on some strange, twilight, post-modern version of television's *Question Time*.

The questions ranged from the inspired – 'Does the soundbite culture mean we are currently facing the death of intelligence?' – to the semi-ridiculous – 'Should people in the music business over the age of 25 be forced to retire and go and work in banks?' – although Blur consistently displayed a humour, wit, intelligence and literacy that seems to be increasingly rare among contemporary pop acts.

Thousands more flocked in their droves, only this time it was away from dull post-punk old fart, Matt Johnson (of The The 'fame') – who was boring the bollocks off all and sundry with his Main Stage performance at 1993's Reading Festival – towards an alternative area where Blur were igniting the *'Maker* stage. Not only did many consider them to be the surprise hit of the festival, Blur's appearance seemed to mark the point where people really started believing in the band once more as a serious force in contemporary music

Slowly but surely, our heroes were gaining on their arch-nemeses, Suede, and – with a successful second album under their belts ('Modern Life Is Rubbish' reached Number 15 in May 1993) – Blur were now providing a live and lustrous alternative to All That Grunge.

'SUNDAY' BEST . . . AND WORST

THE second and third single releases to be from 'Modern Life Is Rubbish' – 'Chemical World' and 'Sunday Sunday' respectively – also attracted several thousand fans, the former record reaching the Number 28 spot

More Piccadilly prancing

in June 1993, the latter climbing to Number 26 in the October.

'Chemical World' was notable in that it contained arguably Blur's finest B-side thus far, the Beatles-circa-'Abbey Road' pretty jauntiness of 'Young And Lovely', a neatly self-descriptive title. The 12-inch also featured the weirdly atonal 'Es Smecht', while on the flipside of the red vinyl seven-inch there reappeared the band's cover version of Rod Stewart's 'Maggie May', the one that they originally recorded for *NME*'s 'Ruby Trax' compilation.

'Sunday Sunday' (backed by a couple of frantic punked-up scrambles through traditional Cockney knees-up sing-songs, 'Daisy Bell' and 'Let's All Go Down The Strand') was also notable in that, albeit isolated from the rest of 'Modern Life Is Rubbish', it revealed several shortcomings in

the band's lyrical/theoretical department.

The song appeared to be a direct rewrite of The Members' ancient punk harangue, 'The Sound Of The Suburbs', a series of fatuous digs by Damon at the domestic, weekend activities of the perennially-despised commuterland, Albarn taking pot-shots at nuclear families who 'read the colour supplement, the TV guide . . . gather around the table to eat enough to sleep'.

It should perhaps be pointed out to Mr Albarn - whose ideas can occasionally seem overly simplistic, half-baked or ill-conceived – that people do things like eat larger meals and wash the motor on Sunday afternoons often for pragmatic reasons – i.e., they don't have enough time during the week – not because they are necessarily mindless androids who act like identikit robots and function on autopilot.

Park Life

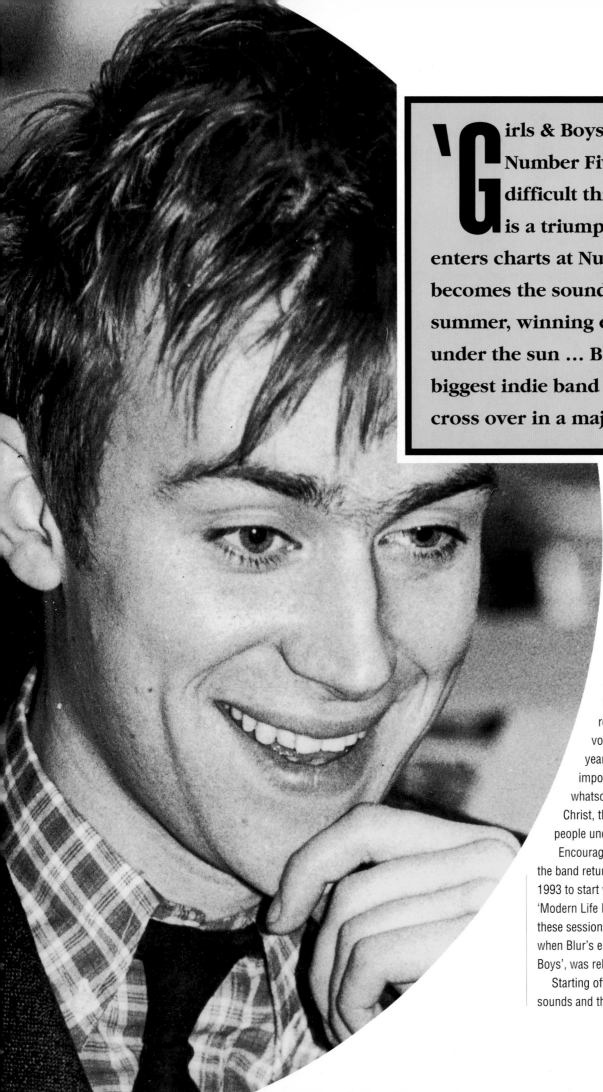

'**G**irls & Boys' enters charts at Number Five ... notoriously difficult third LP 'Parklife' is a triumph ... album enters charts at Number One and becomes the soundtrack of the summer, winning every award under the sun ... Blur become UK's biggest indie band and the first to cross over in a major way ...

'GIRLS' CRAZY

NOTWITHSTANDING the occasional lyrical blunder, by the end of 1993 it was clear that Blur had really got their act together. They were selling records again, they had made a well-regarded album, and the critical/commercial tide seemed to have turned in their favour once more. The readers of *Melody Maker* even voted them best live band of the year. Plus, they had an all-important new rule: no drinking whatsoever before gigs (although, by Christ, they could still drink most people under the table after gigs).

Encouraged by their growing popularity, the band returned to the studio in November 1993 to start work on their follow-up to 'Modern Life Is Rubbish'. The first fruits of these sessions appeared in March 1994, when Blur's eighth single proper, 'Girls & Boys', was released.

Starting off with 15 seconds of toy drum sounds and the kind of eerie, repetitive two-

note synth riff not heard since the electro-pop/white disco glory days of Gary Numan, Visage and OMD, the song quickly rushed into a frantic, maddeningly compulsive series of bleeps, mechanoid guitar riffs, staccato beats and the sound of aircrafts flying backwards at supersonic speed.

'Girls & Boys' was like the best of early Eighties Duran Duran (circa 'Girls On Film') and late Seventies Bowie (circa 'Boys Keep Swinging'), and was approximately seven times more insanely catchy than the most infectious Madness song you care to mention (and, yes, that includes 'House Of Fun'). In short, 'Girls & Boys' was certainly Blur's best single to date, and without doubt one of the finest singles of any released in 1994.

Then there were the words. 'Girls who are boys who like boys to be girls who do boys like they're girls who do girls like they're boys,' went the chorus, which Albarn sung in his best android-Cockney accent. The verse was rather more illuminating, all about 'love in the Nineties' being paranoid – here Damon was once again pursuing his

Latterday Talking Heads

beloved idea of most aspects of life in the modern world being disorientating and alienating – and following 'the herd down to Greece on holiday'.

Damon – in equal parts the mod, the punk and the casual, half student lad and half Essex Man, both the empiric and voyeur – seemed to be reliving his formative adolescent experiences when he would dress up in Farah slacks and Gabicci

Neither could we. The video for 'Girls & Boys' was filmed, appropriately enough, on location at one of these all-drinking, all-shagging holiday resorts, featuring loads of bronzed, moustachioed lads and buxom, blonde, bikini-ed lasses splashing about in swimming pools. The video, together with the single's two great B-sides (another excellent neo-Europop ditty called 'People In Europe' that could easily be covered by

four hicks from the sticks, the sort of record that made you want to burn your other albums because you just didn't need them any more and, besides, they were taking up too much space. 'Parklife' was a true desert island disc.

On 'Parklife', you could hear echoes of Talking Heads' 'Psycho Killer' (on 'London Loves'), Magazine's 'Shot By Both Sides' (on 'Trouble In The Message Centre'), M's 'Pop

Blur had plenty to celebrate in 1994

cardigans and go down to such glitzy London danceterias as the Embassy club in London's West End to watch the mythical Sharons and Kevins indulging in their strange mating rituals. He also seemed to be using the song's lyric to live out his own ideal fantasy holiday experience.

'It's about those sorts of holidays,' he told the *NME*, referring to the 18-to-30 type beanos that we all pretend are beneath us but we all secretly wish we could go on. 'I went on holiday with Justine last summer to Magaluf and the place was equally divided between cafés serving up full English breakfasts and really tacky nightclubs. There was a very strong sexuality about it. I just love the whole idea of it, to be honest. I love herds. All these blokes and all these girls meeting at the watering hole and then just copulating. There's no morality involved. I suppose my mind's just getting more dirty. I can't help it.'

Sabrina or Sonia or Whigfield or somesuch holiday disco diva; and the Teutonic robo-dance of 'Peter Panic') and its clever condom-packet sleeve, made sure that lots of people rushed out to buy 'Girls & Boys'.

And then some. 'Girls & Boys' entered the charts in March 1994 at Number 5. Blur were steadily crossing that great divide between indie favourites and people's choice.

THE BEST OF BLUR

'GIRLS & Boys' was no fluke, either. We know it was no fluke because, in April 1994, Blur issued their third long-playing record, 'Parklife', and it was utterly brilliant, 52 minutes of bliss, almost every one of its 16 tracks – and for once this cliche is more than just lazy hyperbole – sounding like contenders for future single release.

'Parklife' was like a record collection in miniature, the greatest hits of the last three decades all performed and sung by these

Muzik' (on 'Tracy Jacks'), The Jam's 'Eton Rifles' (on 'Parklife'), The Sex Pistols' 'Holidays In the Sun' (on 'Jubilee'), Steve Harley's 'Judy Teen' (on 'Magic America') and Wire's 'I Am The Fly' (on 'Girls & Boys') as well as the now-to-be-expected Madness, Kinks and Pink Floyd influences (Alex James' 'Far Out' was actually the band's first successful attempt to get a psychotic Syd Barrett-ish feel on a song).

There were even two great Middle Of The Road/AOR ballads on 'Parklife' that took the listener back a bit: one lush slow-dance, lighters-aloft weepie called 'This Is A Low' that could have been written by Simon & Garfunkel if the pair hadn't been boring folk musos and had discovered electronic instruments instead; the other, 'To The End', recalling Serge Gainsbourg and Jane Birkin's famously kitsch heavy-breathing epic of eroticism, 'Je T'Aime'. However, never before did accusations of grand musical

Graham's specs never fail to raise a titter

larceny matter less, mainly because Blur's songs had achieved the impossible: they were actually better than their predecessors. 'Parklife' was the kind of album they made back in the old days, way up there with the likes of 'The Lexicon Of Love', 'Dare' and 'Colour By Numbers', the kind of album that features wall-to-wall choruses and hooklines and no fillers.

Lyrically, 'Parklife' represented Blur's second great concept album, this one celebrating life in neurotic modern England. Damon Albarn offered a glimpse of urban paranoia on 'London Loves' ('The mystery of a speeding car . . . the way people just fall apart') and a snapshot of a Great British Custom on 'Bank Holiday' ('John is down the fun pub/Drinking lots of lager/Girls and boys are on the game/All the high streets look the same'). He even penned a quirky paean to

suburban perversion on 'Tracy Jacks' (where the conventional office worker is, behind closed doors, a transvestite).

Elsewhere, there were some to-be-expected sly digs at the United States on 'Magic America' ('Where there are buildings in the sky and the air is sugar-free') and some by-now-typically-Blur-ish, fin-de-siècle, fear of the future-style musings on 'End Of A Century'.

Musically, 'Parklife' featured supremely assured performances from Messrs James, Coxon, Rowntree and Albarn, and was superbly produced by Stephen Street, the latter managing to emphasise all the fabulous little details in the songs: the glorious cartoon harmonies on 'Tracy Jacks'; the gorgeous string sounds on 'To The End'; the squiggly guitar motif, 'hey-hey's and 'oh-ah-oh's on 'London Loves'; the call-and-

response vocals and 'la, la, la, la, la's on 'Trouble In The Message Centre'; the gently lilting harpsichord melody on 'Clover Over Dover', and so on.

Everything was designed and played to perfection on 'Parklife'. It made 'Modern Life Is Rubbish' sound like a debut album in comparison. It made Blur's debut album sound like . . . utter shite, to be honest. It was a pop masterpiece, the benchmark of the year, a giant step forward, a quantum leap for Blur and everyone else. It was, basically, the record that Boo Radleys, Pulp, Oasis, Elastica, Shed Seven, Echobelly and the rest of the Britpop contenders - oh, and Suede - would all have to beat.

'Parklife' was, unarguably, the best album released in 1994. It was also, without unquestion, one of the greatest of the decade. All that and it entered the album best-sellers at Number One, knocking Pink Floyd off the top slot.

Not bad for a group who almost packed it in the year before.

LET US PRAISE

CUE heaps of hysterical praise and rapturous write-ups in every magazine and paper on the planet. The *NME* described Blur as 'the biggest band in Britain' (which was wishful thinking, perhaps – sales-wise, they are still the flame of art school pop' and the *Daily Telegraph* concluded that they had 'mastered the art of British pop'.

Meanwhile, *Big!* described Damon as one of 'the 30 best boys' (the best at what, though?). The *European* applauded their 'British quintessence'. The *Evening Standard* praised their 'ice-cool class'. And *Mojo* called 'Parklife' a 'triumph of arrogance over common sense'. Even the Americans were impressed, *Details* concluding that their one of Blur's faces on it. Inside these august journals, Blur were celebrated, analysed, discussed, dissected, compared, contrasted, put into context, taken out of context, placed atop lists, reviled (by one or two), revered (by everyone else) and generally set up as the most important thing to happen to British pop culture since The Jam, Madness, even – gasp! – The Beatles.

Blur, the whole country seemed to have concluded simultaneously, were the one

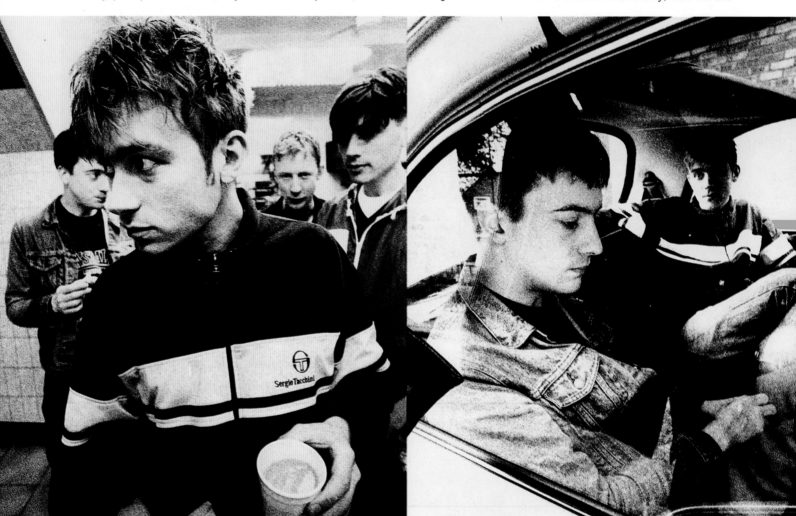

Blur in their natural habitat – cafes and cabs

no match for Simply Red, UB40 or U2). *Select* decided they were the best British band since The Smiths. The *Daily Star* announced that they were the pioneers of the so-called New Mod scene. *Melody Maker* hailed them as the godfathers of the New Wave Of New Wave. *Just 17* labelled them 'the thinking female's crumpet'. The *Observer* announced 'they have rekindled 'youthful blend of intellectual curiosity and self-confidence is riveting' while the usually quite reticent Bible of American Rock, *Rolling Stone*, awarded their album an impressive four stars.

By summer 1994, Blur were everywhere, on serious magazine covers, tabloid covers, broadsheet covers, teen-mag posters – you name it, if it was made of paper, it had all or contemporary group who had managed to appease everyone from factory workers to shop assistants to bank clerks to University graduates, from scuzzy urban crusties to sharp-dressed suburban teens, from acne-ridden delinquents to bearded old fogies. The band with the ice-cool class had crossed – make that transcended – the class, age and sex barriers. (Not the race barrier, though - it has to be said that you don't see many black faces at Blur gigs.) These four boys had captured the ears and eyes of the whole nation.

After several months being bombarded by Blur, all these articles began to look and read the same. Except for the interview with Damon Albarn that appeared in the September issue of *Loaded*, that is. 'Would you give the Queen a good seeing to?' asked *Loaded's* Jon Wilde, a.k.a. 'The Wilde Thing'.

'The first pop star I fancied was Adam Ant, although . . . I never went through that latent homosexual phase. I've always been more of an intellectual bisexual. I like the *idea* of bisexuality.

'I'll say this, though: I'm more homosexual than Brett Anderson,' he added, referring to the Suede man's oft-repeated quote that he's a 'bisexual who's never had a homosexual experience'.

Losing one's virginity . . .

indie, Brett Anderson, Morrissey and The Stone Roses' Ian Brown, who have always shied away from exposing themselves in public, a) because they think it might spoil their private lives or, b) because it might substantially reduce their mystique – Damon was available to be interviewed by anyone and everyone, and ready and willing to broach any and every subject under the sun.

Supremely confident of himself and his own abilities, Albarn lacks the defensiveness

Damon and co have a quick cup o' Rosy Lea before heading down the dogs

'I would have been happy to give her one when she first came to the throne,' was Damon's honest reply.

And it was a crazy rollercoaster ride downhill all the way from there, down along the dark passages of Damon Albarn's sick (that is, normal) psyche. First of all, Albarn and the redoubtable journalist Wilde discussed homosexuality . . .

'We lay down on a very clean bed, did the business, then I walked home and had a nice cup of tea and a fancy bun.'

And so it went on.

This tête à tête was remarkable, not so much for its sleaze quotient, but because it showed that, more than any other major pop star of the last few years – and especially compared with those other great icons of

of many of his peers. He is very open, and he is usually brutally honest. Damon Albarn is the indie Madonna.

GOOD LIFE

THE rest of 1994 was just one continuous blur of successes for Blur. Brit-culture fetishists to the last, in July they held a party for 'Parklife' down at Walthamstow's

Blur's Ally Pally pals – Pulp

greyhound racing tracks. They made triumphant appearances at the Glastonbury Festival in June and at Alexandra Palace in October. In September, it looked as though they were finally going to crack the United States of America when they played a series of dates to the sort of rapturous acclaim they had previously only received in Britain, Europe and Japan.

In September, they were nominated for the coveted Mercury Prize alongside the 'cream of modern music' (allegedly): The Prodigy, Take That, M People, Paul Weller, Therapy?, Shara Nelson, Michael Nyman, Pulp and Ian McNabb. In the event, although Blur were the bookies' favourites to win at 2:1, M People pipped them at the post (some critics of the award strongly suggested that M People's win was more of a political than aesthetic matter).

Then they had two more hit singles. First there was 'To The End', featuring the exquisite Gallicisms of Stereolab's Laetitia

Sadier (there was also a Pet Shop Boys remix of 'Girls & Boys' on the flip that made the song even more Eurodisco-friendly).

Diamond geezer

Then came 'Parklife', co-starring ex-mod icon Phil Daniels, was backed with 'Supa Shoppa', sounding like the ideal muzak for a morning TV quiz show like *Supermarket Sweep*. 'To The End' got to Number 16 in June, while 'Parklife', which seemed to blare from every high street shop, sidestreet office and backstreet workshop through the summer, made Number 10 in August.

There was another single lifted from 'Parklife', 'End Of A Century', released at the end of the year. It came backed with a Country-ish tune sung by Graham Coxon called 'Red Necks' and the bizarre 'Alex's Song' that sounded like an offcut from an old *Pinky & Perky* show.

In December 1994 'Parklife' was Album of the Year in *Q* magazine, they scooped a record four Brit Awards in February '95 (best group, single, album and video) and, finally, they had a book written about them. Could things get any better for Blur?